Power for Yachts

Also by Tom Cox

Motor Boat and Yachting Manual (*Stanford Maritime*)

Power for Yachts

Tom Cox

Stanford Maritime

London

Stanford Maritime Limited
Member Company of the George Philip Group
12 Long Acre   London WC2E 9LP

First published 1975
© 1975 Tom Cox

Set in Lumitype Baskerville 11/12 by
St Paul's Press Limited, Marsa, Malta
Printed by R.J.Acford Ltd.,
Chichester, England

ISBN 0 540 07136 6

Contents

Illustrations

Preface

When writing to give a general insight into a technical subject it can be difficult to define the level at which one chooses to pitch the discussion. This is a technical age and while we may still hear of motorists who do not know where to put the oil in the engine, it can surely no longer be said of most. Hence, in trying to describe basic and long-standing principles of operation in too much detail one may easily become boring rather than illuminating. But in any case this volume does not aim to be a textbook on internal combustion engines at any level; rather it is a short exploration of what is available in marine engines and transmissions for pleasure craft, with some notes on design, installation and performance.

With the foregoing in mind the introduction for those who need to begin at the beginning is only an outline of the general aspect of IC engines and their use in leisure sailing. And for this purpose it was thought suitable to reiterate, with little modification, some of what was included earlier in the *Motor Boat & Yachting Manual*.

Since we are in the process of conversion to metric units of measurement some thought has been given to the figures quoted herein; but it is apparent from manufacturers' literature that to date there is no universal move towards the use of metric units, excepting perhaps in weights, where both imperial and metric are frequently given. Believing that it is necessary to deal with things as they are, no attempt has been made to convert to metric or to quote both imperial and metric units in the text, but the Appendix gives the required conversion factors and these will be of wider and continuing use.

I am most grateful for the material kindly provided by the manufacturers of marine engines and associated equipment both in the UK and abroad, some of whom responded so handsomely that the small space that could be afforded seems poor by comparison.

Cdr. Dick Hewitt, editor of *Motor Boat & Yachting*, has generously allowed me to reproduce some material published earlier in the Journal under my name and I thank him also for reading the MS, which he did with his usual perception. Many of his suggestions have been incorporated. Eric Coltham, staff photographer of *M B & Y*, has made available some of his pictures, as he did for the *Manual*, and I am indebted again for his help.

The drawings, except where otherwise acknowledged, were made by Gerry Wilby and his helpful suggestions as to presentation for clarity have been greatly appreciated.

Tom Cox
Whitstable

Introduction

Most marine engines available for yachts and small working craft are of the reciprocating internal combustion type, that is to say that they burn fuel in a cylinder and the expansion of the gases moves a piston which drives a crankshaft and so rotary movement is obtained. There are other engines using similar fuels which convert energy into rotary movement in a different manner, and a chapter has been devoted to these.

Both petrol and diesel engines may be built specifically for marine applications, but there are many marine conversions adapted from industrial or road vehicle units. In fact many muli-cylinder diesel engines supplied for motor cruisers and small pleasure craft today are marinized versions of units mass-produced for other purposes. It should be noted in passing that the engine which is commonly called a 'diesel' is more correctly a compression ignition (CI) engine since it fires through the heat generated by high compression and not with the aid of a hot bulb or a glow plug. For the sake of clarity and conformity we will continue to call it a diesel.

The horsepower of a marine engine is not given in terms of its capacity as with a car engine, where 1000 cc will rate the car as 10 hp and so on, but by the developed power known as 'brake horsepower' (bhp). This is of course also quoted for car engines but not in reference to engine size; thus a marine engine which is quoted as 5 hp will not necessarily have a cubic capacity of 500 cc (it could be less or more), but in view of the fact that it is developed horsepower which is being given, the engine revolutions per minute (rev/min or rpm) at which it is achieved will also be given, e.g. 5 bhp at 1500 rev/min. This is because the number of revolutions per minute attained under a certain load is the formula for calculation of brake horsepower.

Torque, which is the turning effort and is quoted in lbs/ft, is a valuable indication of the pulling power of an engine and it is quoted also in relation to rev/min; e.g. 50 lbs/ft at 1250 rpm tells the engine speed at which maximum torque is obtained, and increase of rev/min up to the maximum of which the engine is capable will not improve on the torque figure.

Whereas a car may be quoted as doing 30 miles to the gallon, it is not practicable to measure the fuel consumption of a marine engine in that way and it will be stated as fuel by weight or liquid measure used per bhp per hour, e.g. 0.75 pt/hp/hour for an engine developing 5 hp would indicate a consumption of 3.9 pints or just under ½ gallon per hour.

Two-stroke and four-stroke petrol engines are equally popular for marine use. A two-stroke engine produces a power impulse per cylinder for every revolution of the crankshaft and a four-stroke every other revolution. Briefly, small two-stroke units are simple in construction, have fewer moving parts, are light in weight and compact, and as single cylinder units versus their four-stroke rivals probably smoother in operation. However, they are not as efficient as four-stroke engines in regard to power output and fuel consumption. This arises mainly from the fact that with a two-stroke cycle the cylinder has to be scavenged of burned gases and charged with a fresh mixture during the course of the same stroke and some fuel is lost in pushing out the old charge. This is the critical part of two-stroke operation since if exhaust gases are left in the cylinder they will both dilute and reduce the volume of the new charge. Two-stroke petrol engines run on a mixture of fuel and lubricating oil, necessary because the fuel/air mixture circulates in the crankcase before entering the cylinder and is the only means of lubrication.

For equivalent power a two-stroke will cost somewhat more to run since, apart from requiring a rather richer mixture than a four-stroke, some part of every gallon of fuel, varying from about 1:10 down to 1:50 according to the maker's recommendation, will be the lubricant, costing four times as much as the petrol.

Nearly all outboard engines are two-stroke units but there are some four-stroke examples. The power available in such compact packages is an indication of what can be achieved with an engine designed to run continuously at high rev/min. Two-stroke inboard engines can be either high or low rev/min types and one of the most popular and long-standing small inboard engines is in the latter category.

Since acceleration is of little value in a small marine engine, but smooth operation and slow running are important, most of the smaller inboard units used for auxiliary purposes, whether two or four stroke, are fitted with a heavy flywheel which helps to smooth out the power pulses at low speed. Operation at low rev/min so that with or without gearing the propeller is not turning at much more than 1000 rev/min is quite usual and desirable except on very fast vessels: consequently an engine which produces its maximum power and torque at relatively low speed is very suitable for marine use, but as we shall note later this formula cannot be extended much for pleasure craft, where high power and light weight are required.

In the four-stroke cycle separate strokes are utilized for scavenging (exhaust) and charging (induction) and these four strokes in sequence are: induction, compression, power and exhaust. Better breathing, obtained by inducing the mixture into the cylinder with rather more than a complete down stroke (to take advantage of the inertia of the gases), results in a bigger charge and higher efficiency; similarly more complete scavenging on the same principle adds to efficiency. A four-stroke engine can have a much higher compression ratio than a two-stroke unit, and although this fact is not exploited to any extent in marine petrol engines it can contribute to higher outputs for a given engine size.

The valve arrangement for inlet and exhaust on a four-stroke may be either side valve or overhead, and one may expect that if it is built as a small marine auxiliary it will be a low-compression side valve unit, but if it is a marinized car engine it is likely to be overhead valve and to have a much higher compression ratio.

All reciprocating internal combustion (IC) engines may be either normally aspirated or supercharged. In the first case the fuel/air mixture enters the cylinder under atmospheric pressure and in the second it is pressurized so that a bigger charge can be got into the cylinder; this is effected by a compressor which may be mechanically driven by the engine or by a small turbine driven by the engine exhaust gases. Air gets hot when compressed and takes up a larger volume of space; consequently an intercooler may be used between the compressor and the engine inlet in order to reduce the temperature of the charge and thus get the maximum amount of air into the engine for the cylinder volume available. Very few marine petrol engines are supercharged but it is quite usual for the larger diesel engines to have an exhaust driven turboblower.

Excepting the smallest marine engines of less than 5 hp a diesel alternative is now available, and but for what might be called sprint motors in racing craft and the larger sterndrive engines for fast day-boats and short range cruisers, the popular demand is increasingly for diesel power. There are several reasons for this including much higher efficiency (which tends to be disregarded or not known by many potential users), and lower fuel cost and fire risk – both of which are generally appreciated. The availability of high output, lightweight diesels for pleasure craft is a spin-off from the development of light, multi-cylinder units for road vehicles and boat owners may well be grateful for the greater scope it offers them in powering their craft.

While there is much to be said for the multi-cylinder diesel engines, the case for the smallest diesel auxiliaries vs petrol is not quite so strong. A lot will depend on the type of boat, but perhaps more attention should also be given to the nature of its use. An auxiliary sailing yacht will normally have need of its engine for only short periods, and because of the shape of a sailing hull there will frequently be only limited space in which to install an engine and its fuel tank; lightness is also of importance if performance under sail is to be maintained, and further, minimum vibration is essential in a light hull. All of these considerations indicate a petrol engine as being far more suitable; but in spite of this, and the much higher first cost, many diesel engines are installed in quite small sailing boats. Many owners appear to make the choice purely on the grounds of lower fire risk.

If there is room for argument over the respective claims of small petrol and diesel units there is little doubt that the multi-cylinder diesel engine has most points in its favour. The necessarily high compression ratios needed (more than twice that of most petrol engines) which can give rise to very rough running in single cylinder engines is greatly reduced with multi-cylinder units, and it will be apparent that the problem is halved if the engine has only two cylinders. With three or four in line, six in line and V configurations major imbalance is overcome and the residual noise and vibration is that which results from the nature of ignition and combustion requiring extreme cylinder pressures. But this also is amenable to treatment by anti-vibration mountings and noise insulation. High cylinder pressures call for extra robust design all round and it is this which makes the difference in weight between petrol and diesel engines of the same horsepower.

Most of the marine diesel units adapted from road vehicle engines have a four-stroke cycle, but in the field of engines designed for marine use there are both two-stroke and four-stroke examples and the two-cycle diesel engine may claim some advantages over the four-stoke which are not realizable in a two-stroke petrol unit.

The fundamental difference between the operation of diesel and petrol engines is that although the strokes have the same purpose, whether two cycle or four, only air is drawn into the cylinder by the diesel and the fuel is injected at high pressure at or near the top of the compression stroke; the heat engendered by high compression is sufficient to ignite the fuel-injected air charge without the aid of a spark. Petrol engines with fuel injection do not have abnormally high compression ratios and they still employ spark ignition. There are diesel engines fitted with glow plugs to assist starting but they are not in use once the engine is running.

A quick review follows of the major points for different units to power yachts and similar small craft.

The inboard two-stroke petrol engine is simple, low in cost but available only in the low power range suitable for small sailing auxiliaries.

Four-stroke petrol engines are available as small auxiliary units and also, with multi-cylinders, in sizes suitable for main propulsion in fast dayboats and short range cruisers. They are most efficient in regard to power output for weight and size, but the high cost of petrol makes the larger motors very expensive to operate.

Small diesel engines from about 6 bhp are made as auxiliaries or for launches and small workboats. The smallest units are generally single cylinder, frequently with notable tendencies to vibration; neither this nor the additional weight is of great consequence in a workboat but it can give rise to problems in a small, lightly built vessel.

Multi-cylinder diesel engines are being standardized to an increasing extent by the builders of all classes of boats, and apart from the high performance given by petrol units, which must remain an attraction for some purposes in spite of the cost of their fuel, the diesel is now the most attractive proposition for a motor cruiser. A wide power range is available and their economy helps to offset first cost. This fuel economy is also valuable in that it increases the range of a cruiser without resort to abnormal tankage.

Outboard engines are discussed in a later chapter but meantime it may be said that many people prefer them for auxiliary use on small sailing vessels and they also power the greater proportion of runabouts and weekend cruisers. Power ranges from $1\frac{1}{2}$ up to 150 bhp and they are by far the most compact power packs available. In the USA they are also used extensively as the main propulsion on sizeable cruisers and big dayboats; in the UK petrol engines of high horsepower are more likely to be found in conjunction with sterndrives as the alternative to diesels in fast, light cruisers.

1. Inboard Petrol Engines

As noted in the general remarks on reciprocating IC engines, the choice in petrol units lies between a two or a four stroke unit, but as far as inboard engines are concerned this choice is only available in the low power range suited to auxiliary use and the powering of small launches. It is possible to find an exception to most rules, e.g. the Crescent Marine Drive Unit of about 40 bhp, but two-stroke inboard engines popularly marketed in the UK do not exceed 12–15 bhp. -

Characteristics

Engines can have very different characteristics although operating on the same cycle and developing a similar amount of power; some of the basic contributory factors are capacity, weight and designed rev/min, but there are many others which influence performance. Obviously manufacturers decide on the design parameters to suit the chosen role for their product, but equally obvious is that they may have rather different ideas as to what is best for the job. Thus – and without inferring any superiority to either – the Stuart Turner ST4 produces 12 bhp at 1650 rpm while the Seafarer Mk 2 delivers the same power at 4000 rpm. But it should be noted.that the former while turning in a more leisurely manner to produce equal power has nearly three times the capacity and is also more heavily built. So close consideration should be given to the purpose in mind, that is, the kind of boat and its use. Is it of light or heavy displacement? Will the normal service required of the engine involve continuous running over long periods or will it have only occasional duties? Defining factors of this kind and relating them to the performance and specifications of apparently suitable units will help to indicate the best engine for the job.

Looking at four-stroke engines in this low power range we see that the same remarks can apply in regard to characteristics and variables within the same power requirement. Taking as example the Brit 12/55 with a capacity of 1420 cc which turns out 12 bhp at only 1200 rpm, we can compare this with the Albin 0.22 of 800 cc which gives 12 bhp at 1600 rpm. The difference in rev/min is not so marked as in the two-stroke example but there is a considerable difference in capacity and also in weight. However, in general, and compared with car units, small marine engines are not expected to produce spectacular bhp in relation to capacity. The aim is longevity with continuous running at or near maximum rev/min.

Power/Weight Ratios

Power requirements for inboard petrol units of more than 25 bhp are almost wholly met by multi-cylinder four-stroke engines and many of these will be based on well tried car units. What might be called the graduate class in inboard petrol engines is represented by the highly developed units made for use with sterndrives by the makers of the larger outboard engines. The Mercruiser engines producing up to 255 bhp for sterndrives and 350 bhp for conventional or V-drive transmission are in this group.

It should be noted that the rev/min at which maximum power is obtained is very much higher than is the case with most of the low power engines, but there is also a dramatic reduction in weight for the brake horsepower developed.

Torque, Power, Fuel Consumption

Torque is the pulling power of an engine; it is measured in lbs ft and is shown as a curve plotted against the engine revolutions (rev/min). The peak of the curve indicates the maximum torque or turning effort which may be obtained from that unit.

Power developed, which is rate of doing work, is also indicated as a curve against engine rev/min, and since the figures are obtained by loading the test engine with a brake it is referred to as brake horsepower (bhp). The manufacturer's recommended maximum rev/min will also be the speed at which the rated bhp is obtained.

The peak of a torque curve can occur at a different place in the engine speed range according to design of the unit, but it still remains a curve which ordinarily drops before maximum bhp is attained. For some purposes this is no drawback, e.g. with a road vehicle a high torque is useful low down in the speed range in order to start easily under load and also for hill climbing, but it is not needed to the same extent when running at higher road speeds. With a boat the situation is rather the reverse since the engine will normally be run at a steady speed for long periods and the cruising rev/min of the engine will be near the top end of the speed range. Thus if the engine is of the kind which develops its power at high rev/min it is desirable to have good torque in that region also. In this sense it might be considered that it does not matter at what engine speed the unit achieves its maximum power provided that the torque characteristics are compatible. But in practice high rev/min has no advantage for normal marine use since the propeller efficiency will generally impose a limit on rev/min which has to be met by the use of a reduction gear with higher speed engines.

An engine which is designed specifically for marine use – as are some of the smaller petrol units – may produce its power and have good torque at quite low speed, e.g. 1000–1200 rpm, which is more acceptable from the point of view of propeller efficiency, but as we have noted earlier it does so at the expense of a larger capacity and weight, and although of course it may be inferred that longevity should be enhanced because of this, the implication of increasing size and weight does not make extension of the formula viable for pleasure craft. Thus for more power without a penal increase in weight there must be higher engine speeds and this situation is met by the type of petrol unit which has already been developed for road vehicle use. Consequently petrol units available in the middle and higher power ranges are more often than not marinized versions of such engines. But as we have noted, because the unit was designed for a different purpose the torque curve may not be ideal for some marine use. That need not be a notable disadvantage where speed is required rather than slogging power under load, except that it should be observed that the rev/min for economical fuel consumption towards the top end of the range is normally much nearer the rev/min at which maximum torque is attained rather than maximum power, and that fuel consumption will ordinarily rise with bhp to reach its highest at full power. This is a circumstance of which some advantage may be taken for cruising; by running the engine at a speed nearly coincident with maximum torque and lowest fuel consumption the best efficiency is obtained in driving the boat (Fig. 1.1). But propeller matching can also come into this.

Without wishing to overstate the obvious, it may be inferred that a

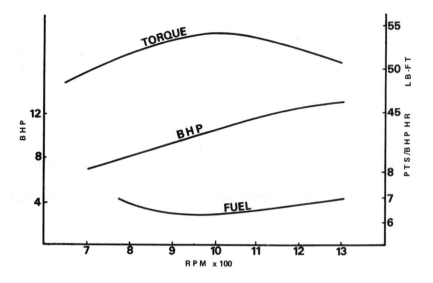

1.1   Torque, power and fuel consumption curves for the Brit 12/55 marine petrol engine

heavy displacement boat can usefully employ a heavy engine with a propeller chosen to take more advantage of the torque available, but a light displacement or semi-displacement boat for which a wider speed range is required may beneficially use a high speed unit which produces more power for weight, and the propeller will be chosen to enable the engine to reach its maximum power rev/min. The situation does not remain so well defined with the larger displacement boat which requires more power from a petrol unit, because only medium or high speed engines are available in the higher power range.

From the foregoing it may be seen that the smaller, low speed petrol engines are very suitable for auxiliary yachts and launches up to the overall length for which their power makes them useful, and beyond this a multi-cylinder, high speed unit with a reduction gear can be employed, but at this stage a diesel unit may well be considered. Light motor craft such as fast launches and weekend cruisers with semi-displacement and planing hulls will have the multi-cylinder high speed petrol engine if an inboard unit is preferred, but in this area there is also the alternative of the high power outboard engine, or the inboard/ outboard.

It may be of interest to note that there has been some difference between the UK and the USA in the acceptance of petrol engines for larger craft. It may be that the accustomed use of high powered and rather thirsty petrol engines in American automobiles influenced the attitude, but it is not unusual for quite large motor vessels to have petrol units of suitably high power installed in spite of the fuel consumption. They may be used with conventional transmission or stern-drives and they are lighter and quieter and have perhaps a more brisk performance than a diesel unit, but the development of lightweight diesel engines in the UK has meant that for some years now they have displaced the petrol engine for medium as well as large motor cruisers – including those with the ability to plane.

Carburation

The supply of a suitably regulated fuel/air mixture to a petrol engine, whether two-stroke or four-stroke, calls for similar carburation although the mixture may take a very different route to the combustion chamber. In the conventional two-stroke petrol motor it will be induced into the crankcase before being passed up via a transfer port to the cylinder. Thus the upward movement of the piston is used to draw the fuel mixture into the engine and the downward movement pushes it into the cylinder so that it may both scavenge the exhaust gases from the previous stroke and charge the cylinder at the same time for the next. Apart from the fact that the two-stroke engine fires every time the piston reaches the top of its stroke, other obvious differences are the need to have a gas-tight crankcase and a lubricant in the fuel/air mixture.

The oil incorporated in the fuel mixture is the sole means of lubrication for all of the moving parts of the engine, and of course it works on a total loss system since most of it passes up into the cylinder with the petrol and air and is burned. Adherence to the manufacturer's recommended oil/petrol ratio is most important: too much oil will result in a dirty exhaust and possibly oiled-up plugs; too little will be rather more serious for the wearing surfaces of the engine may suffer by way of worn bearings, cylinder scoring and loss of crankcase compression. Besides a general loss of efficiency, starting can be affected badly by poor crankcase sealing through wear, since less fuel will be drawn into the engine, and less still transferred up into the cylinder.

Two-stroke engines can be particularly baffling sometimes with regard to starting, and although experience tends to indicate that the problem does not arise to any extent when starting from cold, there are times when a hot engine seems to refuse all persuasion and in these circumstances it is perhaps best to give up temporarily so that you can both cool off! The very simplicity of the unit seems to defy any change in circumstance which could cause such occasional difficulty, but assuming that there is a healthy spark, the first recourse is to examine the sparking plug for fouling. As mentioned, unless properly regulated, the means of lubrication is liable to cause dirty plugs, and also various petrol additives may assist in causing fouling and whiskering of the electrodes. Some owners make a practice of keeping sets of clean plugs at the ready to guard against this, and also to get going again quickly should the engine cease to idle when hot.

Some two-stroke engines have a drain plug so that old oil and over-rich mixtures can be cleared from the crankcase. Occasional attention here is well worthwhile in removing another possible cause of plug fouling and difficult starting.

The air/fuel mixture required by petrol engines when warmed up is in the order of 15 : 1 but every engine type will have its own requirements; some are thirstier than others for the same output. Consumption can be varied to a considerable extent by the nature of use. An engine from which smart acceleration is required will need a temporarily richer mixture for that purpose; some carburettors have an accelerator pump to take care of this. Full throttle running will also use more fuel (Fig. 1.1) but some experiment is possible, in order to get the best economy, with those units where a steady running speed is anticipated. However, very lean mixtures make for higher engine temperatures, and taken too far a weak mixture can cause burning of plug points – and more seriously, burning valves and seats. Indications of a very weak mixture are spitting back through the carburettor, flat spots and hesitation when the throttle is opened, high exhaust manifold temperature, and if the exhaust pipe is disconnected the flames will be blue-white. Sparkplug electrodes tend to whiteness.

Rich mixtures may give lumpy running at low speeds and hunting, and in the case of a four-stroke engine, black smoke from the exhaust. Exhaust manifold temperatures will be lower than normal and if the pipe were disconnected the flames would be seen to be orange-red. Plug electrodes are sooty.

Carburettors fall into two main categories: the fixed choke variable vacuum and the variable choke constant vacuum – or more simply, the fixed jet/choke and the variable jet/choke types (Fig. 1.2). In both cases the fuel supplied from the tank is kept at a predetermined level in the

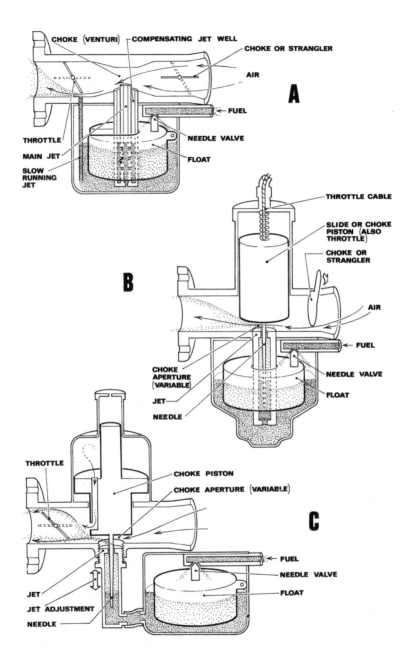

1.2   Carburettor types: *A* fixed jet, *B* variable jet, *C* SU type variable jet

bowl of the carburettor by means of a float operating a needle valve. The level of petrol in the jets is of course the same as that in the bowl which, as indicated, serves as a self-compensating reservoir. Some variation in mixture strength can be made by adjusting the level of the fuel but the main means of adjusting the mixture is by the use of carefully calibrated jets which come into operation on demand with increasing engine speed. The flow may also be compensated by secondary jet wells and air bleeds. In the case of the variable jet, only one is employed, the size of the orifice being controlled by a tapered needle which is withdrawn from the jet with increasing throttle opening.

In all cases whether fixed or variable jet, the fuel is drawn out by the passage of air at high speed across the top of the jet orifice; the lower pressure so caused over the top of the jet causes the atmospheric pressure in the carburettor bowl to push the petrol out. Thus it is normally important that the small air bleed hole in the top of the carburettor float chamber is kept open, although some designs, such as the diaphragm carburettor on the Vire 7, may be made leak proof.

In order that the maximum pressure difference over the top of the jet is attained, the jet whether fixed or variable, is arranged so that it projects into the barrel of the carburettor in the area of the choke. The choke is a restriction (fixed or variable) in the barrel of the carburettor, the purpose of which is to increase the air speed at that point. The arrangement is also known as a venturi, and it should not be confused with the choke or strangler which is used to restrict air going into the carburettor and thus give a richer mixture for starting. Some variable jet carburettors provide a starting mixture by lowering the jet body.

Control of the amount of fuel/air mixture going through the carburettor into the engine is by a butterfly (throttle) valve on the engine side of the venturi. Thus the engine will run with increasing speed as this is opened, allowing more mixture to be drawn into the inlet manifold.

For slow running, a fixed jet carburettor will have a separate, small jet which is open to the engine when the throttle is nearly closed and this normally has an adjustment for an air bleed so that the mixture strength may be varied to suit a small throttle opening – sufficient to permit the engine to tick over. In the variable jet/choke carburettor the slow running mixture is adjusted by varying the height of the jet body in relation to the needle valve, or by altering the setting of the needle in the choke piston if there is no adjustment for the jet body. The variable choke normally takes the form of a piston which can slide up and down across the choke passage in the carburettor barrel, so either increasing or decreasing the size of the aperture, the pressure and the admission of air. The tapered jet needle is fixed to the bottom of the piston and rises and falls with it, thus the quantity of fuel as well as the amount of air is regulated. The lift of the piston and jet needle may be effected either mechanically or by reduction of pressure in a chamber over the top of the piston. Small variable jet carburettors have a mechanical control via a Bowden cable and the piston also acts as the throttle valve. Larger, multi-cylinder engines, if fitted with a variable jet/choke carburettor, will probably have the pressure controlled type. The variation in pressure to operate the piston is effected by having an air passage from the carburettor barrel on the engine side of the choke to the chamber over the top of the piston. Variation in inlet manifold pressure which occurs when the throttle is opened makes operation of the piston entirely automatic (Fig. 1.2 C). The fixed jet/choke carburettor is rather more popular for multi-cylinder engines.

Obviously mixture strength in fixed jet carburettors can only be altered significantly by changing the jet for a larger or smaller one, but with the variable jet type alteration can be made by adjusting the needle or jet height or fitting a needle with a modified taper. If the carburation is badly out of tune with an instrument of the latter type it is possible to zero the setting of the jet needle and choke piston and start again from scratch – but it is advisable to check first that the piston is moving freely as this is a possible source of trouble. To zero the setting raise the jet body to its maximum height (if an adjustment is incorporated); remove the piston and needle from the carburettor body and slack off the needle holding screw until the needle is just a push fit in the piston; withdraw the needle slightly and carefully re-insert piston and needle into the carburettor; press down gently on the piston so that the needle is pushed up into it by contact with the jet orifice and continue pressure until the piston reaches the bottom of its travel; remove the piston with the needle very carefully so as not to disturb the setting, and tighten the needle holding screw; reassemble. The nut which adjusts the height of the jet body will need to be slacked back slightly to provide a starting mixture and from thence it can be adjusted either way to give a smooth tickover when the engine is warm. This setting will serve through the whole engine speed range unless a particular characteristic is required as may be obtained by fitting a needle with modified taper. For variable jet carburettors without a jet body adjustment, the needle and piston height at rest (throttle closed) is varied by the cable adjustment on top of the carburettor body.

Starting

The richer mixture which is required for starting a petrol engine is obtained either by use of a choke or strangler which restricts the amount of air (the fixed jet carburettor) or by increasing the size of the fuel jet temporarily (variable jet/choke carburettor). The smaller variable jet carburettor may have a strangler instead of an adjustable jet body.

In most cases the action of the strangler or a movable jet is effected manually, but it can be automatic either by means of vacuum from the induction manifold or it can be electrically controlled. Most car owners will have experienced the effects of over-choking in attempting to start from cold and the remedy is the same for a boat engine. The choke needs to be opened, and the throttle too, to its fullest extent while turning the engine over, so as to get the maximum amount of air into the cylinders and thus dry out some of the surplus fuel. Obviously an automatic choke is unable to know what it ought to do in these circumstances since its reaction awaits the conditions which have not yet been achieved, i.e. the engine has not yet started so the choke will remain closed. Thus foiled by the benefits of progress the only action open to you is to open the throttle wide, but do not continue to turn the engine until you have flattened the battery. If after the suggested treatment it will not start, it is likely that the plugs are thoroughly wet with fuel and they will need to be removed and dried out before making further attempts. For the purpose of this note we are of course assuming that the ignition is functioning properly.

Leaving aside positive faults such as lack of fuel, spark or compression, condensation is more often than not the cause of difficulty in cold starting when the engine has been left overnight and it is this which leads to over-choking in vain attempts to get the engine to fire. Persistence can only lead to worsening the condition and so it is best to turn attention to the distributor cover, which should be wiped out with a clean cloth or absorbent tissue; wipe the outside also and give the same treatment to the insulated body of the spark plugs. If the engine refuses to fire after this the plugs should be removed, dried out with a flame or any convenient heat (do not get them too hot) and then lightly wire-brushed before replacement.

A contributory cause to poor starting in adverse conditions is failure to keep the plug electrode gaps within the stated limits. Starting problems are frequently remedied if the gaps are set to the maker's lower figure.

Petrol/Paraffin Fueling

Most low compression petrol engines will run on paraffin when warm, using the same carburettor and settings as for petrol. The features to observe are that the power output will drop significantly and that it is necessary to provide a small separate tank for petrol for use when both starting and stopping. It will be appreciated that unless petrol is in the carburettor before the engine is stopped it will not start again until the paraffin therein has been displaced by the more volatile fuel. It is necessary therefore to switch over in good time so that the system, from tanks on, is clear of paraffin before the engine is stopped.

In regard to fuel, it may be said that the higher the compression ratio of the petrol engine, the higher octane it will use, and as a general indication two-stroke and small, side valve, four-stroke engines will run on two star petrol while multi-cylinder OHV engines will need either three or four star fuel. A point in passing concerning petrol fuel tanks is that highly volatile fuels such as petrol can give rise to a large amount of water condensation in the fuel tank through changes in temperature and humidity. This condensation will gather in the bottom of the tank and will thus be drawn preferentially through the system. The effect is emulsification in the carburettor which will clog the jets and this, with the water content, will make starting extremely difficult and the unscheduled stop highly likely. It is best therefore to leave the boat over any extended period with tanks which are either full or absolutely empty.

Valve Timing

From the owner's point of view the valve timing on a four-stroke engine whether side or overhead valve is not adjustable – except inadvertently by the amount of clearance on the tappets – and it is not recommended that this should ever be anything but the maker's specification. Clearances other than those recommended will cause a fall-off in performance and this is particularly so of high speed multi-cylinder engines which run with timing which gives a considerable amount of valve overlap. Burning of exhaust valves and seats can occur if the tappet clearance is not sufficient to permit proper seating for the required amount of time. Adjustment should follow the recommendation precisely, and not merely in the matter of clearance. If the maker says the tappets should be adjusted with the engine cold, make sure it is so, because if it is not you will get an entirely different setting from that intended. When using the feeler gauge to check the clearance remember that it should only be a firm slide fit; if it requires much effort to move it you have probably been opening the valve with its aid. Needless to say, it is easier to adjust both inlet and exhaust valves on a cylinder when it is at the top of its compression stroke rather than to try to locate the exact back of the cam for each individual valve.

Lubrication

Two-stroke lubrication has been mentioned in connection with car-buration, but the lubrication of a four-stroke unit as with a car engine is an entirely separate function and because of this it is rather easier to ensure that the various parts receive oil at both the required pressure and viscosity. The circulation system normally conforms to general IC engine practice with a wet sump from which oil is drawn to be pumped under pressure to the principal bearing areas, further lubrication being achieved by surplus oil from these being thrown with the rotation of the crankshaft and other moving parts. It is usual to incorporate a filter in the system and with a petrol engine this will generally be of the replaceable cartridge type. Larger engines will be fitted with oil coolers, the heat exchange being effected by raw water cooling or inclusion in a fresh water cooling system.

Oil circulation may be by plunger pump on the smaller engines, but multi-cylinder units more frequently have gear-type pumps and operate at higher pressures. A gauge may be fitted or an oil pressure warning light. A hydraulic gearbox will have its own pressure lubrication system with filtration and cooling.

Provided that the maker's recommendations are followed as to oil and filter changes and the grade of oil there is little to go wrong with the lubrication of a modern engine. The maximum pressure will be controlled by a relief valve on the pump and the expected pressures when running at various speeds, e.g. slow running or cruising, will be quoted by the makers. Any significant variation from these should be investigated. Low pressure is most likely to be the cause of concern and supposing the engine is known to be in reasonable condition in regard to bearings a fall-off in pressure could otherwise be brought about by overheating, a choked filter or other obstruction, a low level of oil in the sump, leakage, or the wrong grade of lubricant.

Ignition

Ignition for petrol engines can be by separate magneto, flywheel magneto or one or more coils. In any case a current is supplied by either the magneto or the battery to excite a primary (low tension) coil. Collapse of the current in this coil, which is effected by the opening of the contact breaker, causes a high tension current to be induced into a secondary coil (which has a much larger number of windings) and this provides sufficient voltage to cause a spark at the plug electrodes. It will be observed that the timing of the high tension spark is controlled by the timing of the contact breaker opening in the low tension field. To prevent arcing across the points, that is a tendency for the current to try to continue to flow through the contacts while they are opening, a condenser is fitted which bridges the contacts (Fig. 1.3).

Contact breaker opening is effected by a rotating cam driven by the engine. Since the points must open to produce a spark at every plug in sequence multi-cylinder engines will have cams with more than one lobe, e.g. a four-cylinder four-stroke engine which will complete its sequence of firing on all four cylinders in two revolutions of the crankshaft will need a cam with four lobes which is driven at half engine speed so that it distributes a spark to each cylinder in one revolution; the distributor rotor being mounted on and turning at the same speed as the contact breaker camshaft.

In some small inboard engines and particularly in outboard engines a flywheel magneto is incorporated. This generates current by having magnets which rotate with the flywheel and the coils are stationary. The cam lobe for the contact breaker is on the crankshaft. But many of the bigger outboard engines now have capacitor discharge (CD) ignition, which will be discussed later.

Adjustment to set the amount by which the points open is normally made by moving the earth side of the contact breaker points nearer to or farther away from the moving contact. The breaker points should be set to the opening recommended (which may be 0.010–0.018 in) not only to produce the best spark but also because any significant variation will affect ignition timing. Arrangements for timing correctly vary and besides the number of degrees about top dead centre (TDC) quoted in the engine's manual there will also be some visual indication either on the flywheel or perhaps on an auxiliary drive pulley at the other end of the crankshaft which will indicate either TDC or a timing mark or both. In the case of a four-stroke engine it is necessary to make sure that the piston is on the right stroke when timing the ignition to

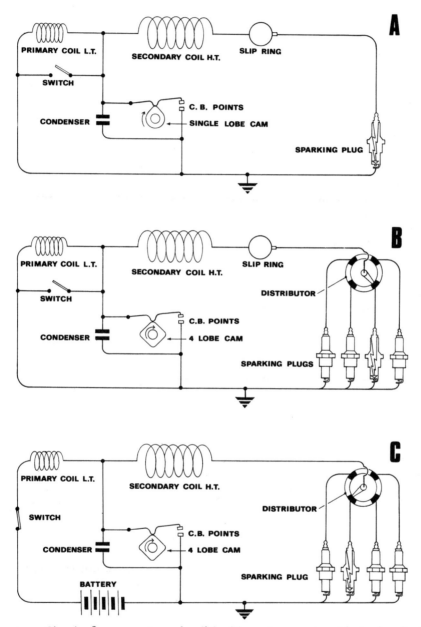

1.3 Circuits for magneto and coil ignition: *A* magneto with single cylinder engine, *B* magneto with multi-cylinder engine, *C* coil with multi-cylinder engine

the flywheel mark, i.e. at the top of the compression stroke; and in the case of a multi-cylinder four-stroke engine the appropriate cylinder as well as the right stroke must be ascertained.

For ordinary check or adjustment on a multi-cylinder unit the correct cylinder can be noted by removing the distributor cover and turning the engine over until the rotor indicates the appropriate segment (plug lead). The maker's instructions will inform on the sequence of firing and procedure.

Should the timing be entirely lost, perhaps through incautious withdrawal of the distributor drive shaft or removal of the mangeto coupling, and there is no instruction book to hand to advise on sequence or timing, there are elementary means of retrieving the situation. First the sequence of firing can be noted by reference to the direction of movement of the rotor and the length and situation of the plug leads even if they are disconnected; if they are still connected there are no problems in that direction, but if you are uncertain, No. 1 cylinder should be put at the top of its compression stroke and then turning the engine slowly note the sequence of the opening and closing of the valves, i.e. No. 1 will have both valves closed when you start and the next cylinder to have both valves closed will be the next in order of firing, and so on. Having established the sequence so that you can reconnect the plug leads correctly (reference distributor rotation), the next thing is to time one cylinder. The TDC mark on the flywheel will probably refer to No. 1 but if otherwise it will be marked. So assuming it is No. 1 cylinder, get it at the top of its compression stroke (both valves closed) with the flywheel indicating TDC. Re-insert the distributor drive shaft or connect the coupling having first turned the rotor to a position opposite No. 1 segment of the distributor head and ensured the contact breaker points are just about to open with the advance mechanism, whether manual or automatic, *fully retarded*. In this position the least movement of the ignition advance mechanism should open the points and that, in the absence of more precise knowledge from your manufacturer's instruction book, will be found to be a satisfactory setting for most engines.

A point to be noted in reference to ignition current is that when switching on two quite different things occur depending on whether a coil or a magneto is fitted. In the case of the former, switching on connects the coil to the battery; with the magneto, however, switching on actually disconnects the low tension winding from earth (Fig. 1.3). In both cases the action enables the LT winding to become energized – the coil by taking current from the battery and the magneto by rotation (generation). If when dealing with magneto ignition there is an absence of spark, the recommended first move is to disconnect the switch lead and re-test because if there is any shorting in the switch through moisture or any other agency the magneto will be rendered 'dead'. It is the sort of thing which can happen easily when, as in the case of many small auxiliaries and launches, the switch is mounted in the cockpit, or in an incompletely protected position. A quick spark check with coil ignition can be made by disconnecting the coil-distributor lead at the distributor end and holding it near any convenient earth, e.g. the cylinder block. Flicking the contact points open with the finger nail should produce a spark at the end of the lead. The ignition should of course be switched on.

Cooling

Marine engines, whether two- or four-stroke, petrol or diesel, may be either air or water cooled. With all the water available it might be thought that there is no field for air-cooled units, but although, speaking broadly, air-cooling does not find so much favour for larger engines, the smaller diesel units are frequently offered with a choice of either cooling system. The fact that the smaller units, if water cooled, normally employ raw (sea) water with its known corrosive properties through the whole system, may be some inducement to air-cooling. Other attractions are an absence of skin fittings apart from the exhaust, and freedom from freezing precautions if the boat is in service during the winter. Having said that, it should be acknowledged that the majority of petrol engines, large and small, are water cooled. For the larger units the drawbacks of raw water usage are overcome by the employment of heat exchangers so that the actual cooling of the engine is by fresh water in a closed system. The fact that many of the units available with higher outputs are based on automobile engines which are almost universally water cooled but not designed to withstand a great deal of corrosion in the system makes the use of a heat exchanger a rather more attractive proposition (Fig. 1.4).

The heat exchanger may take the form of a small engine-mounted tank which is part of the freshwater circulation system. A continuous flow of seawater pumped through tubing immersed in the tank takes the heat from the fresh water and thus cooling is effected without enduring the effects of direct seawater circulation. An alternative arrangement is for the freshwater system to incorporate tubing or

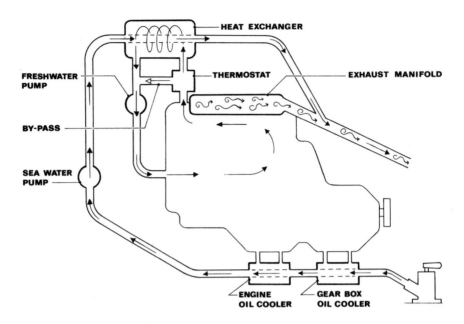

HEAT EXCHANGER

FRESHWATER PUMP

THERMOSTAT

EXHAUST MANIFOLD

BY-PASS

SEA WATER PUMP

ENGINE OIL COOLER

GEAR BOX OIL COOLER

1.4   Heat exchanger freshwater cooled engine with direct seawater cooling of engine and gearbox oil and water injection exhaust

some other form of exchange surface on the bottom of the boat where it is in direct contact with the flow of seawater. In the first arrangement water pumps are required for circulation in both parts of the system; in the latter obviously only the fresh water is circulated.

Whether direct seawater or a heat exchanger system is employed for

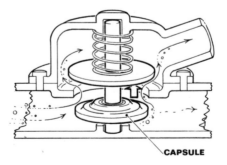

CAPSULE

1.5   Water thermostat showing capsule operated valve

cooling a thermostat should be incorporated so that a reasonable range of engine temperature is maintained and a quicker warm-up from cold is made possible. The thermostat is a valve which operates to short out the cooling surfaces of the system when the engine temperature drops. It is actuated by a small metal bellows which reacts to change in temperature by altering its length; the movement is utilized to operate a disc valve over a bypass port in the water system (Fig. 1.5). Failure can occur through puncture of the bellows or gumming up by deposits which restrict its action. The cause of an unwarranted rise in engine temperature can be checked by temporary removal of the thermostat from its housing if that is where suspicion falls, but simpler causes such as clogging of the seawater inlet should be investigated first.

Silencing

Exhaust silencing can take a variety of forms, e.g. a direct discharge below water, a water cooled discharge above water, or a chamber-silenced dry discharge above water. The first method is nearly universal for outboard engines but sometimes seen on very big motor yachts with diesel engines. The third method provides too much hot metal inside the boat, all of which needs lagging; consequently unless the engine is air-cooled the second of the above systems is that most popularly employed. The use of seawater for cooling and contracting the gases is convenient since, excepting air-cooled units, it is already being circulated either in a direct raw water cooled system or through a heat exchanger. The exit for the seawater can therefore be made via a water cooled silencer or some part of the water from the system may be bled off for the purpose (Figs. 1.4, 1.6). The two main considerations for a water injected exhaust are that it shall not be possible for the water to flow back into the engine via the exhaust ports and that all the materials employed in the system will stand up to the corrosive effect of hot gases and seawater.

In auxiliary yachts the engine will frequently be situated below the waterline, in which case a swan neck pipe which rises up from the engine well above water level before descending to its outlet is essential, or an exhaust riser to a water injection box should be fitted (Fig. 1.6). A drain cock is incorporated at the lowest part of the swan neck system to take care of any water which might collect there through a surge of water up the tailpipe. For motor vessels the height of the engine ex-

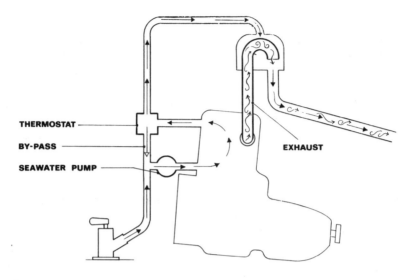

THERMOSTAT

BY-PASS

SEAWATER PUMP

EXHAUST

1.6   Direct seawater cooling

haust is generally such that it is only necessary to make sure that there
is sufficient fall in the pipework to discourage any flowback at the
maximum angle at which the boat may be pitched by the seas.

Starters

Where starters are fitted on the engines discussed in this chapter (and
if not standard they will be available as an option) they will be of the
electric motor type with a self-engaging pinion in the case of most
engines, but on some of the smallest units the equipment has a dual
role as both starter motor and generator. It is hardly possible for the
latter type to jam since it has a V-belt drive which is always engaged and
is either driving or being driven, but the conventional car-type starter
motor with an inertia pinion (Bendix) can sometimes jam in the engaged
position in which case the torque of the motor from rest is generally
insufficient to turn the engine. It will be found that the end of the
armature which is approachable is squared off so that it may be turned
with a spanner. By turning this in the direction opposite to its usual
rotation the pinion can be 'unwound' out of mesh with the flywheel
ring. The helix on which the starter pinion is mounted should never be
lubricated as this can cause sticking either in or out of mesh.

The current required from the battery by the starter motor is very heavy and consequently the cables are kept as short as possible to reduce the voltage drop. This means that the starter switch, which must be in the cable run, is normally remotely controlled. The wires from the starter switch on the engine control panel can be quite light since they are only required to switch enough current to operate a solenoid and this in turn operates the heavy duty starter switch in the starter relay. If the control switching is suspect it is sometimes possible to operate the relay directly by hand by removing the cover over the end of the solenoid, or the two cable terminals can be shorted (Fig. 1.7).

Battery charging current is supplied by the engine driven generator, or more popularly nowadays by an alternator which is able to supply more current at a lower speed than a DC dynamo. Apart from rectification the charging system is much the same as that for a DC generator and it is automatically controlled by an automatic voltage control (AVC) unit which reduces the charge as the battery condition improves. In the case of twin engine installations twin charging and paralleling of the circuits is possible (Fig. 2.16). These considerations on electric starting apply equally to diesel engines, but larger diesel units may have compressed air or hydraulic starters.

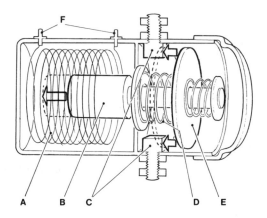

1.7 Starter solenoid: *A* solenoid coil with terminal connections *F* from ignition switch, *B* armature, *C* starter motor current terminals, *E* disc contact, *D* return spring

General Construction

Besides improvements in lubrication and more durable wearing surfaces, perhaps the major step forward in recent years has been the
increasing amount of stiffness which has been built into petrol IC
engines. The smaller single and twin-cylinder marine units have always
been good in this respect through comparatively heavy build, but there
was room for improvement in multi-cylinder units.

Crankshafts, which even in four-cylinder engines used to depend
upon only a bearing at each end, plus – later – an extra one in the
middle, now have a main bearing between each throw, thus removing
the whip which was one of the principal hazards to sustained high
speed operation. Crankshafts and bearing journals have similarly been
increased in size in relation to capacity; crankcases are no longer
hollow shells but rigidly webbed to fit them for a dynamic as well as a
static role. The power now being developed by the lightweight car
engines which are the basis of many of the marine units mentioned
here almost wholly depends upon high rev/min made possible by
greater rigidity and improved balance. True, the user of a marine
engine may not have a particular need for power units which run at
high rev/min, but were he to try to acquire comparable power by other
means it would cost him a great deal more in weight and money.

Ancillary equipment, because of its functions, tends still to be the
source of occasional trouble, but it is likely that most of this could be
traced to inattention at the appropriate time. Plug electrodes and
contact breaker points are both consumable in the sense that they need
replacement at intervals which are frequent compared with the life of
the engine. Brushes in starter motors and generators, glands in water
pumps, and belt drives are all items which, in addition to oil and air
filters, need occasional attention and replacement if their reliability
is to be consistent with the basic unit's capability.

An advantage given to the owner of a road vehicle engine based unit
is that many of the ancillary items will be obtainable as service exchange
spares, and probably at reasonable cost and availability.

Design Examples of Inboard Petrol Engines

The design examples which conclude this chapter have been selected as
far as possible to illustrate some differences in approach to similar
requirements, but a sufficient number of types is included in an attempt
to make them representative of what is available at present.

AUXILIARY AND LAUNCH ENGINES

Vire 7   Single cylinder, air-cooled two-stroke. Fitted with marine gearbox and 2:1 reduction as standard, also 12V starter-generator with voltage regulator and switchgear. The exhaust manifold is water cooled to improve scavenging. Max. bhp 7 at 2500 rpm. Weight 115 lbs. (Fig. 1.8)

Stuart Turner P66   Twin cylinder, water cooled two-stroke. Available with or without electrics, and with reverse and reduction gear or centrifugal clutch. Max. bhp 10 at 1650 rpm. Weight with reverse/reduction gear 278 lbs. (Fig. 1.9) *Other models*: R3M 1½ bhp, P6 5 bhp and ST4 12 bhp. All water cooled.

Seafarer Mk II   Twin cylinder, water cooled two-stroke. Fitted with marine gearbox as standard, also Siba Dynastart starter-generator. Max bhp 12 at 4000 rpm. Weight 136 lbs.

Brit Imp   Single cylinder, water cooled four-stroke. Marine gearbox fitted as standard. Optional electrics with 12V Siba Dynastart. Max. bhp 5 at 2000 rpm. Weight 150 lbs. (Fig. 1.10) *Other models*: Sprite 10 bhp and Brit 12/55 12 bhp.

Watermota Super Shrimp   Single cylinder, air-cooled four-stroke. Fitted with 2.5:1 reduction and variable pitch propeller as standard also 12V starter-generator. Max. bhp 7 at 3500 rpm. Weight with stern-gear 98 lbs. (Fig. 1.11) *Other models*: Shrimp 3 bhp, Sea Wolf 50 bhp, Sea Tiger 78 bhp and Sea Leopard 98 bhp.

Lombardini LAM 300   Single cylinder, air-cooled four-stroke. Marine gearbox and 2:1 reduction as standard. Max. bhp 6 at 3600 rpm. Weight 88 lbs. *Other models*: LAM 490 9 bhp.

Volvo Penta MB 10A   Two-cylinder, water cooled four-stroke. Illustrated (Fig. 7.5) with Sailboat Drive (MB10A/100S). The standard MB 10A is fitted with a reverse gearbox and a starter-generator. Max. bhp 15 at 2000 rpm. Weight 258 lbs or 310 lbs with sailboat drive. *Other models*: MB 20B (for paraffin) 26–42 bhp, BB 115B 115 bhp and BB 170A 170 bhp.

Wickstrom W2   Two-cylinder, water cooled four-stroke. Supplied with v.p. propeller and sterngear. Max. bhp 12 at 1500 rpm. Weight 140 lbs (Fig. 1.12). *Other models*: W1 6 bhp, W3 22 bhp.

Renault RC 15   Two-cylinder, water cooled four-stroke. Mechanical gearbox. 12V Dynastart starter-generator. Alternator optional. Max. bhp 15 at 1500 rpm. Weight 297 lbs. *Other models*: (type no. indicates hp) RC6, RC8, RC25, RC40.

RCA Dolphin MkVII.   Two-cylinder, water cooled two-stroke. Electric starting. Max. bhp 12 at 3200 rpm. Weight 90 lbs.

Tempest Vedette Mk 8   Four-cylinder, water cooled four-stroke. Supplied with either PRM 140 hydraulic gearbox or conventional manual box. Electric starting and generating equipment. Max. bhp 25 at 3000 rpm. Weight with hydraulic gearbox 475 lbs. (Fig. 1.13)

MAIN PROPULSION ENGINES

Fisherboy 1100   Four-cylinder, water cooled four-stroke. Illustrated with Hydrive hydraulic gearbox. Manual box available if required. Starter and alternator fitted as standard. Max. bhp 41 at 4500 rpm. Weight (with Hydrive gearbox) 326 lbs. (Fig. 1.14) *Other models*: Fisherboy 1600 60 bhp.

Watermota Sea Wolf   Four-cylinder, water cooled four-stroke. Available with hydraulic or mechanical gearbox or sterndrive. 12V alternator and starter as standard. Max. bhp 50 at 6000 rpm. Weight with hydraulic drive and 2:1 reduction 410 lbs. (Fig. 1.15) *Other models*: Sea Tiger 78 bhp, Sea Leopard 98 bhp.

Volvo Penta BB 115B   Four-cylinder, water cooled four-stroke. Supplied complete with Volvo reduction/reverse, Borg-Warner hydraulic gearbox. Alternator and electric starting as standard. Max. bhp 115 at 5000 rpm. Weight 440 lbs. (Fig. 1.16)

Mercruiser 255   Eight-cylinder V-8, water cooled four-stroke. Raw water or freshwater cooling. Hydraulic gearbox. Alternator and full electrics as standard. Four choke carburettor. Max. bhp 255 at 4800 rpm. Weight 917 lbs. *Other models*: Mercruiser 225, 225 bhp; Mercruiser 325, 325 bhp.

1.8 Vire 7

1.9 Stuart Turner P66

1.10   Brit Imp

1.11   Watermota Super Shrimp

1.12   Wickstrom W2

1.13   Tempest Vedette Mk 8

1.14   Wortham Blake Fisherboy 1100

1.15   Watermota Sea Wolf

1.16   Volvo Penta BB 115B

2. Diesel Engines

It is recorded that the first British diesel lorry was powered with a converted Gardner marine engine. No one can say today that the truck industry has not repaid its debt, for worldwide, most of the marine diesel engines sold in the medium power range are based on automotive or industrial units. A large number of the smaller engines employed as auxiliaries also have relatives in industry. For the boat owner, therefore, a range of choice is given at a price which could not be approached if his was the only market.

In considering the advantages of diesel vs petrol engines for pleasure craft, one of the first persuasions in favour of the diesel is likely to be the reduction in fire risk, but to see only this attribute as the basic and clinching argument is to ignore other factors which deserve more recognition from potential users. The relative thermal efficiency of petrol and diesel engines is approximately 24% and 35% respectively – giving both the benefit of equally good examples. Hence there is an initial advantage to the diesel of nearly 50% over the petrol unit in the economy with which it utilizes its fuel for a given load. This factor does not arise from any particular design feature but from the fundamental reason that higher compression ratios give higher efficiency, and the compression ratio of a petrol engine is strictly limited by the volatility of its fuel. The additives in premium grade petrol are mostly there to reduce this inclination to pre-ignition and thus permit somewhat higher compression ratios to be used.

Another advantage basic to the diesel is its ability to produce high torque, and this, as discussed in the previous chapter, is what makes the propeller turn under load. From the foregoing it is clear that even supposing the petrol engine used a fuel which was no more inflammable than diesel oil, the diesel would still have a high claim to priority for marine use; when the further dimension of turbocharging is added it has a very high claim indeed.

As indicated earlier, the operating cycle of a two or four stroke diesel is the same as that of a petrol engine, the major difference being that whereas in the carburettor petrol motor the fuel is drawn in with the air, in the diesel only the air is aspirated, the fuel being injected just before the top of the compression stroke. It is because of the different method of fuel supply that the diesel two-stroke can be made rather more efficient than its petrol counterpart, and in fact it can yield more power for its size and weight than a four-stroke diesel unit. However, the two-stroke may be a little more costly to produce and although there are some excellent examples its four-stroke rival has a large share of the pleasure boat market.

Power/Weight Ratios

As with petrol engines, power/weight ratios for diesels improve when the rated output is achieved at higher rev/min, but even lightweight high speed diesels do not turn over at the speed of multi-cylinder petrol units, and in any case the more robust construction called for by higher compression places the diesel at a weight disadvantage by comparison with petrol engines of similar power. It should be noted, though, that development is tending to narrow the gap.

TABLE 1

Engine	Petrol Diesel	Cycle	bhp	rpm	Weight lbs	Power/weight ratio (approx.)
Watermota Sea Leopard	P	4	84	5500	430	5.1 lbs/hp
Ford 2402	D	4	79	3600	783	9.9 lbs/hp
Foden FD4	D	2	84	1800	1430	17.2 lbs/hp
Lister HWR6M	D	4	88	2200	1845	20.8 lbs/hp

Some examples of power/weight ratios for marine diesel engines compared with a typical petrol unit of approximately similar power. All weights include an addition of a reverse/reduction gearbox.

Torque, Power, Fuel Consumption

Both two and four stroke diesels in the high speed category can produce good torque characteristics, and most are able to show high and flattish curves indicating the ability to work hard through most of the speed range and near the top end where, in a marine installation, they will get most of their running time (Fig. 2.1).

As with petrol engines, the power (bhp) rises sharply with increasing engine rev/min and from the middle of the speed range the fuel consumption will normally accompany this. It should be noted though that the diesel engine of whatever type is inherently more modest in its fuel demands than a petrol unit, owing to its higher thermal efficiency.

The British Standard defines bhp measurement for diesel engines as the rev/min multiplied by the torque (in lbs ft) divided by 5250, and this definition is also used in North America.

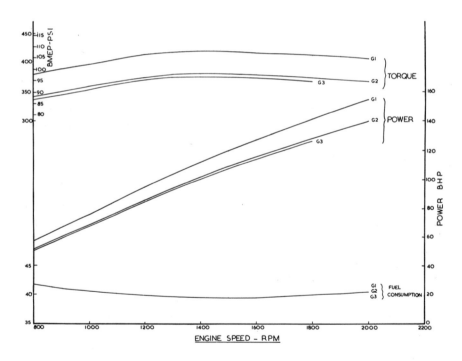

2.1   Torque, power and fuel consumption curves for the Foden FD.6 marine diesel engine of 147 shp

Combustion

Diesel engines may be designed to employ either direct injection, in which the fuel is injected into the top of the cylinder (Fig. 2.2), or indirect injection by which the fuel is injected into an antechamber where the charge is ignited and combustion initiated prior to propagation in the cylinder (Fig. 2.3). There have been many different designs for pre-combustion cells, the research being encouraged by the less violent and more prolonged combustion characteristics which are a feature of indirect injection. There are, however, some disadvantages apart from a rather more involved cylinder head design. Starting is generally more difficult 'due to the lower compression ratio and some assistance is necessary for cold starts, such as a glow plug in the pre-combustion chamber. Very cold starts with a direct injection engine may be assisted by a heated fuel spray injected into the inlet manifold.

For some years there has been a move to direct injection for multi-cylinder units and although some manufacturers make engines to both designs it seems that at present the indirect injection engine only has continuing popularity on the Continent. As may be inferred the current supremacy of the direct injection engine had depended greatly on improved combustion chamber and injector design, the hub of the matter being the nearness to which the designer gets to complete atomization of the fuel and its thorough distribution in the air charge. To this end various swirl-promoting cavities may be incorporated in the cylinder or piston head and inlet valves are also masked sometimes so as to contribute to air swirl. As an instance, the toroidal cavity which may be seen in the design of some piston heads is incorporated to produce a vertical rotary air movement as the piston approaches the cylinder head on the compression stroke; at the same time a masked inlet valve or offset port may be used so as to have imparted a horizontal rotary movement to the air when it was brought into the cylinder, thus there is an interaction between bodies of air moving in different planes and it is concluded that atomized fuel injected into this will be thoroughly dispersed through it (Fig. 2.4).

The design of the injector may be single or multiple hole and the orifice(s) may be at various angles; similarly, the mounting of the injector in the cylinder head may be at any angle from vertical according to combustion chamber design.

The valve arrangement of a four-stroke diesel is similar to that of a petrol unit in that it has both inlet and exhaust valves operating through similar valve lift mechanism, but whether a two-stroke diesel has any

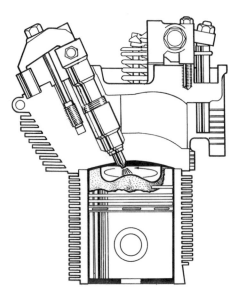

2.2   Direct injection (*Deutz*)

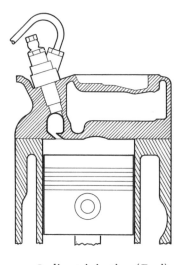

2.3   Indirect injection (*Ford*)

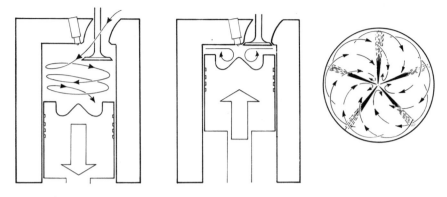

2.4   Two-way air swirl promoted by angled inlet port and shaped piston head (*Scania*)

poppet valves in the cylinder head depends upon the method which is used for scavenging. Crankcase compression is not necessary since only air is used for charging and scavenging and this can be more efficiently supplied by a low pressure blower. The scavenging system may be cross-flow, loop, or uniflow (Fig. 2.5). As will be seen, the uniflow system requires an exhaust valve in the cylinder head whereas the others have exhaust as well as inlet ports in the cylinder walls. In the uniflow design the gases are not required to change direction; the air coming in under pressure from the ports in the cylinder wall flows up the cylinder

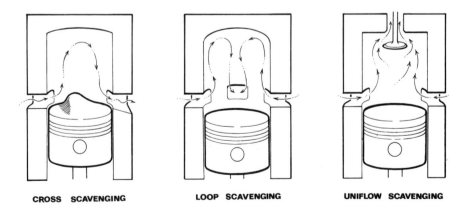

CROSS SCAVENGING   LOOP SCAVENGING   UNIFLOW SCAVENGING

2.5   Two-stroke engine scavenge systems

and in doing so propels the exhaust gases before it so that they exit via poppet valve ports in the cylinder head. Cross-flow scavenging, as implied, has inlet and exhaust ports in opposite walls of the cylinder and a shaped piston crown deflects the incoming charge into the top of the cylinder where it displaces the exhaust gas causing it to discharge through the opposite port. Loop scavenging depends upon angled inlet ports in the cylinder wall and a shaped cylinder head. The inlet ports are on nearly opposite sides of the cylinder and the incoming charge is directed upwards where assisted by curvature in the cylinder head it propels the exhaust gases down and through a port or ports between the inlet apertures. Cross-flow scavenging is much used in petrol two-stroke engines, but diesel two-cycle engines normally employ either loop or uniflow systems, with the emphasis on the latter (Fig. 2.6).

Fuel Pumps and Injectors

The fuel pump and injectors are dealing with very small quantities of fuel at each stroke and great precision is needed in the manufacture and maintenance of this equipment since even these pinhead drops of fuel oil must be accurately varied in amount to regulate the power of the engine. Multi-cylinder engines may have an in-line fuel pump with a plunger for each injector, or a distributor type pump may be fitted which has only one pump chamber supplying the injectors sequentially via a rotating distributor (Fig. 2.7). A combined pump/injector for each cylinder is sometimes used, the GM Detroit Diesel being an example which has a constant stroke, variable spill pump built into each injector (Fig. 2.8A).

The amount of fuel supplied by the pump is varied by a governor operated by mechanical, hydraulic or pneumatic means to provide sensitive regulation of engine power according to the throttle opening. A maximum power stop is incorporated so that the engine cannot exceed its safe output, and a minimum speed stop controls tickover. On some engines an emergency air shut-off is also fitted so that the unit can be shut down irrespective of the fuel feed.

Fuel metering is accomplished in the multiple plunger in-line pump by means of variable delivery pistons (plungers) which while having no alteration to the length of stroke may be rotated within the pump cylinders; in one example a helical edge cut into the skirt of each piston coincides with an oil delivery port in the wall of the cylinder

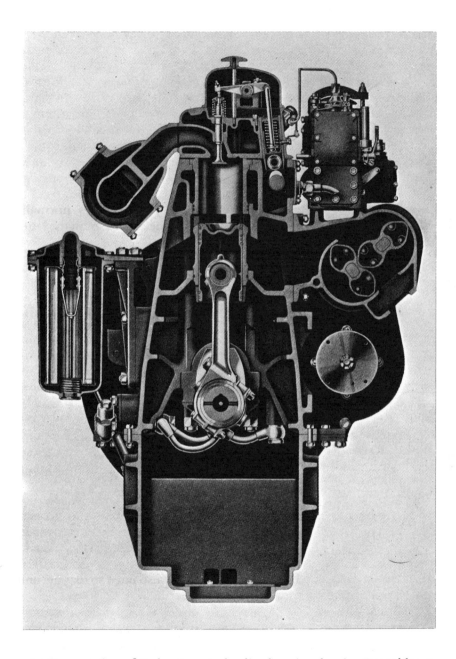

2.6   Cross-section of Foden two-stroke diesel engine showing Roots blower for air charge and uniflow scavenge system

2.7   Distributor type CAV fuel pump on Perkins 6.354 diesel engine (*Eric Coltham*)

for a period determined by the degree of rotation of the piston, thus the port is uncovered for a greater or lesser time and the quantity of fuel pumped to the injector may be varied from nil to the full power requirement. The distributor type pump has a metering valve which accomplishes the same purpose. In a multi-cylinder 'in-line' fuel pump the pistons are controlled in unison by a rack which is in contact with the actuating pinion on each piston; alternatively, a peg and lever arrangement may be used, the peg on each piston being moved by a lever which is common to them all.

The fuel injection pump is fed from the fuel tank by a supply or fuel lift pump which may be a diaphragm, gear or plunger type operated

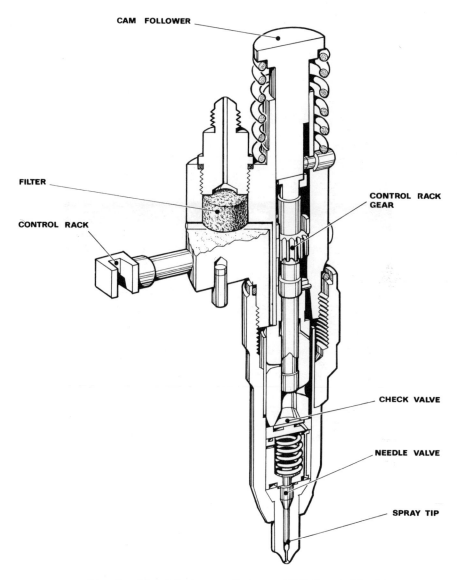

CAM FOLLOWER

FILTER

CONTROL RACK

CONTROL RACK GEAR

CHECK VALVE

NEEDLE VALVE

SPRAY TIP

2.8A   Combined fuel pump/injector (GM *Detroit Diesels*)

mechanically, or the diaphragm pump could be electrically operated. Some of these will have a priming lever which can be manually operated and most have a small inlet filter, but this is secondary to the fuel line

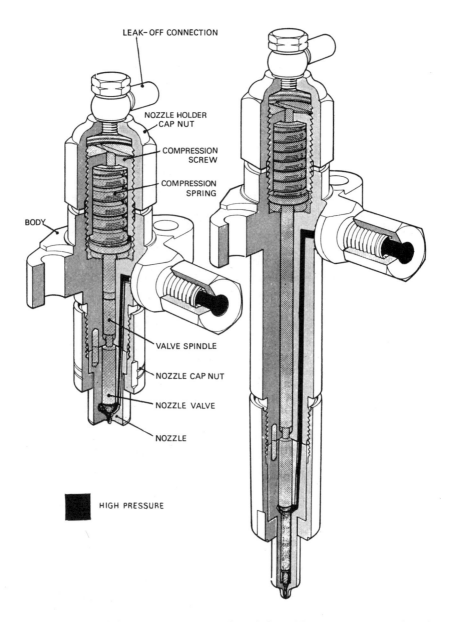

LEAK- OFF CONNECTION

NOZZLE HOLDER
CAP NUT

COMPRESSION
SCREW

COMPRESSION
SPRING

BODY

VALVE SPINDLE

NOZZLE CAP NUT

NOZZLE VALVE

NOZZLE

HIGH PRESSURE

2.8B   CAV injectors. Conventional on left and long-stem type right.

filters, one or more of which is incorporated in the supply line between the tank and the supply (lift) pump. The importance of these filters cannot be overstressed in view of the very small clearances in both the fuel injection pump and the injectors so that they deliver exactly the minute quantity of fuel dealt with at each stroke.

As indicated above, injectors may vary considerably in design but all those used in high speed diesels are of the closed type with a cut-off valve to improve atomization and prevent dribble; this feature is a part of the function of the non-return valve in the injection pump, which is designed so as to rapidly reduce pressure in the delivery pipe on closing thus causing the injector valve to snap back onto its seat and give a clean cut-off to the injected fuel. Injection is in the form of a single or multiple spray of sufficient force to overcome the pressure in the cylinder and mix with the compressed air charge. Direct injection engines normally employ multi-hole injectors. A sharp termination to the fuel spray is most important as even a small amount of excess fuel can cause rough running and a great deal of smoke. If the condition is allowed to continue it may also give rise to carbon deposits on the injector valve and contamination of the lubricating oil.

It will be noted from the description of the non-return valve function that when fuel is pumped into the pipe connecting with the injector, both the pipe and the injector are already charged with fuel and the new pulse from the injection pump puts sufficient pressure behind this to overcome the spring holding the injector closed and cause a 'jerk' of oil to be injected into the cylinder. From this it will be appreciated that if for any reason an injector feed pipe is disconnected at either end, entrapped air might prevent the injector from working when the pipe is reconnected. In view of this the injector union nut should not be tightened until the engine has been turned over a few times so that air or aerated fuel may be expelled; the union can then be tightened.

Perhaps this is the point where it may be suggested that whereas with a diesel there is rather less to go wrong than with a petrol engine, there is also less that the average owner can do if it ceases to function. In fact beyond ensuring that the fuel supply is unimpeded and unadulterated there is nothing much that can be done without the aid of a skilled mechanic and some special workshop tools. The whole of the injection equipment is made to such fine limits and is so dependent on correct calibration and cleanliness during assembly that dismantling is not recommended except as a last resort, consequently complete spare injectors should be carried when voyaging far from home. However, for those left without options the following might be of some use –

remembering that apart from the checks on fuel supply, filters, etc which are clearly within the owner's capability, what is advised re injectors may be better effected by skilled attention whenever possible.

A complete failure to run should be investigated by a check through the fuel system, starting with a look at or dip check on the fuel tank and a check on the position of the fuel cock. The next stage is to loosen the union nut on one of the injector pipes. If no fuel is ejected when the engine is turned over the supply should be verified as follows. Disconnect the inlet pipe on the injection pump and turn the engine over. If no fuel comes out, check back along the line towards the tank through the fuel lift pump and filters by loosening or disconnecting unions until you strike oil. The location of the obstruction should then be apparent.

If fuel is present at the injection pump inlet, reconnect the union, loosen the air vent screw and turn the engine over. If any air bubbles emerge continue turning until they cease and unaerated fuel is being delivered, then tighten the vent screw.

Supposing that there is still no fuel at the injector union(s) the injector pump delivery valve may be stuck, but it is not likely that this would happen to all of the valves simultaneously on a multi-cylinder pump and other injector unions should be loosened for trial. If there is no fuel at the injector unions when you have made these checks it could be one of a number of fuel pump faults none of which are likely to be within your means of identifying or rectification, except that the throttle linkage should be checked for operation and also the minimum speed stop to ensure that it has not slacked off so as to shut off the fuel for idling.

If there is fuel at the injector union(s) then the fault must be in the injector(s), but again, a complete failure to run due to an injector fault can only be likely with a single cylinder engine. If a faulty injector is positively indicated it may be removed from the engine and carefully dismantled on a clean work surface, using the utmost care not to bend the valve stem on withdrawal. The valve should come out of the nozzle body easily, but if it is sticking and does not respond to treatment with penetrating oil it may be left to soak in paraffin. It should be noted that the valve and nozzle body are fitted together as a pair and should be replaced as such if damaged. Supposing the valve can be withdrawn, both it and the nozzle body should have their various grooves and passages cleaned with brass wire scrapers and prickers; this includes the spray nozzle. The valve seat, if carboned, can be cleaned off with a brass scraper, and a brass wire brush is generally useful during these operations. Never use steel wire or a drill for cleaning any part of an injector. Give a final wash in paraffin and then dry and polish with a non-fluffy cloth before re-assembly. A set of injector cleaning tools may be purchased, and for those sailing far from home they could be a good investment for emergencies.

To locate a faulty injector on a multi-cylinder unit the engine should be run at idling speed and the union nut on each injector slackened in turn. If an injector is working properly the change in engine note and vibration will be noticed immediately. If slackening the union makes no difference to the running of the engine the faulty injector has been identified. Some injectors are fitted with a test pin which rests on the nozzle valve and projects from the top of the injector; on others the spring adjusting screw may be drilled so that a short length of wire can be inserted to touch the top of the valve. In both cases the object is to be able to feel the pulsations of the valve when the engine is running. If the action is irregular it could be due to a broken valve spring, misadjustment of the spring tension, or the valve might be sticking.

An injector may be checked for delivery by removing it from the engine and reconnecting the pipe from the injection pump; the engine should then be turned over either by hand or with the starter motor, with the decompressor (if fitted) open. In the case of multi-cylinder engines without decompressors the union nuts on the other injectors should be slackened so that the engine cannot start.

Care should be taken not to get the hands or any bare flesh in the path of the fuel spray since it will be at a pressure which can penetrate the skin. Besides being immediately painful, neglect could cause blood poisoning. The affected part should be bathed immediately and medical attention obtained.

Fuel system spares:
1 Replacement fuel filter element
2 Set of sealing and O rings for each filter
3 Spare vent screws for pump and filters
4 Set of high pressure injection pipes (with both ends plugged to prevent entry of dirt)
5 Spare set of fuel injectors of the right type, correctly set for the engine, together with a set of seating washers if required
6 Spare banjo bolts and washers for back leak pipes and low pressure pipes
7 A set of the correct spanners for the job
8 Polythene bags to contain fuel oil and element when changing filter
9 Barrier cream for hands

Fault Diagnosis

Incorrect idling and max. speed	Loss of power / Poor consumption	Uneven running, misfiring	Excessive exhaust	Difficult starting	CAUSE
					SYMPTOM
				X	1 No fuel
				X	2 Stop control
				X	3 Starting procedure
X		X		X	4 Air in system
X	X			X	5 Fuel restriction
				X	6 Fuel contamination
				X	7 Cranking speed
				X	8 Starting aid
	X	X	X	X	9 Injection timing
X	X			X	10 Feed pump
X	X			X	11 Blocked return pipe
X	X	X	X	X	12 Poor compression
	X			X	13 Exhaust system
X	X	X	X	X	14 Fuel atomization
	X				15 Fuel tank vent
	X	X		X	16 Firing order
		X			17 HP pipe restriction
X	X	X		X	18 High pressure leaks
	X				19 Low pressure leaks
X					20 Idling speed incorrect
X	X				21 Max. speed incorrect
X	X				22 Accelerator linkage (throttle)
		X			23 Engine mounting
		X			24 Vibration
		X			25 FI pump mounting
X	X	X	X	X	26 FI pump

This chart is by courtesy of CAV. It provides a useful summary of symptoms and possible causes of operating faults. Both this and the suggested list of fuel systems spares are from the Lucas CAV booklet on *Diesel Fuel Injection Equipment for the Boat Owner.*

CHECK

Fuel level
In run position, linkage free
Is it correct?
System vented, all joints and unions air tight
Filters and pipes clear
Fuel free of water, dirt, ice, wax
Correct lub. oil. Battery, starter and cable connections
Correct functioning. Fuel supply and electrical connections
Pump to engine timing
Pressure
DPA pump back leak, return to tank and filter vents free
Cyl. compression. Air intake clear. Injector seats. Valve clearances and timing
Unrestricted
Injectors – type, setting, condition, sealing, tightened down
Vent unrestricted
HP pipes fitted in correct order
HP pipe bores not kinked or reduced at nipples
HP pipe joint tightness
Fuel pipes for leaks
Engine idling speed setting
Engine maximum no load setting
Lever loose on pump, reaches stops, linkage wear
Mountings are tight
Vibration not transmitted from elsewhere
FI pump drive and mounting bolts tight
If all else fails remove FI pump and send for specialist check

Turbocharging

The development which has had the most startling effect on power/
weight ratios in recent years is undoubtedly turbocharging. The idea
of improving power output by accelerating and increasing the volume
of air entering an engine is quite old – mechanically driven super-
chargers were much the vogue on prewar racing car engines – but the
problem with mechanically driven blowers is the power they themselves absorb when driven at high speed and also in the design of a
satisfactory drive which will stand up to the sort of speeds demanded.
All engine-driven ancillary equipment must inevitably take away from
the output of the engine, but the extent to which this may occur is perhaps not very apparent. The advent of the exhaust-driven blower has
changed the picture considerably for the diesel engine, and although
it is never possible to get something for nothing the turbocharger
gives a great deal for very little. It is possible to obtain a 50% increase
in power compared with a naturally aspirated engine of the same
capacity; the cost in extra weight is quite small, and fuel consumption
can be improved. Besides giving an improvement in thermal efficiency,
the turbocharged diesel is of particular interest for marine use because
it operates best under continuous high speed and load conditions – the
circumstances which prevail for most of the time in the operation of
motor cruisers and fast powerboats.

To date turbocharging has been applied mainly to engines for the
medium to large pleasure power yachts but it would seem that the
advantages may also be available soon for smaller units. The Perkins
T4.108M engine showed an increase in power of 32% with a weight
increase of only 4%. With particular attention to fuelling and turbo
matching very high efficiencies may be achieved. The Perkins V8.510M
which produces 160 shaft horsepower turns out 235 shp in the form of
the TV8.510M for pleasure craft applications.

In function the turbocharger is very simple, although a lot of design
attention has to be given to balance, distortion and lubrication. A small
turbine wheel is driven by the exhaust gases and on the same shaft there
is a centrifugal blower (Fig. 2.9). In practice it is found that with careful
matching the turbine adjusts itself to engine breathing requirements at
various speeds. Since the compression of air causes heating of the
charge it is usual to have an intercooler between the turboblower and
the inlet manifold and this can be water cooled as part of the seawater
circulation system, which is independent of the freshwater circuit and
gives a greater temperature difference.

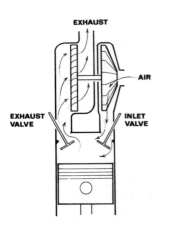

EXHAUST

AIR

EXHAUST
VALVE

INLET
VALVE

2.9   Exhaust-driven turbocharger

Diesel engines are not renowned for quiet operation and the turbo-charger adds a characteristic whine to the general noise output, but experiment with air intake and air cleaner design can do much to ameliorate the problem. Referring again to the TV8.510M engine, the air cleaner and intake developed for this removed the high frequency whine and reduced the overall noise by 3 dB (Fig. 2.10).

Lubrication

Engines running under continuous load, as they do in motor cruisers, require heavy duty lubricants with thorough filtration and, as far as possible, controlled maximum temperature. The manufacturer's recommendation should always be observed as to type of lubricant and frequency of oil and filter changes. Multi-cylinder engines have provision for oil cooling either by a seawater cooled exchanger or, in the case of air-cooled engines, a radiator through which some of the cooling blower air stream is directed. The Foden two-stroke diesel has its oil cooler in the freshwater circulation system and by this means the thermostat also controls the lubricating oil temperature.

Impurities entrained in the lubricating oil may be removed either by filtration or centrifugal cleaning; in the first the filter element can be of the replaceable or the washable type, in the second the oil under pressure is used to rotate a centrifuge, the outer cylinder of which can be cleaned of the accumulated deposits as required (Fig. 2.11).

As with petrol engines an oil pressure gauge is provided on multi-

2.*10*   Air intake cleaner and silencer developed for the Perkins TV8.510M
235 shp marine diesel. (*Author*)

cylinder units and if a hydraulic gearbox is fitted it will have its own
gauge. Any fall-off in pressure from the maker's limits when the engine
is at normal running temperature should be investigated immediately.
The more obvious possibilities are leakage, low oil level in sump, or
choked filters.

Cooling

The cooling arrangements for a diesel engine are much the same as
those for a petrol unit and similar systems will be found in practice.
Engines may be air or water cooled and water cooling may be by raw
(sea) water circulation, or by heat exchanger with a closed freshwater
system (Fig. 2.12). In general only the smaller single and twin cylinder

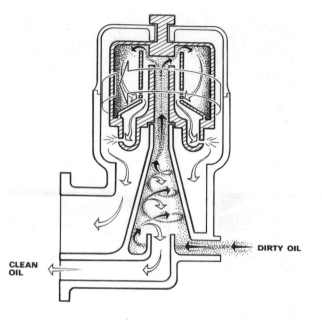

CLEAN
OIL

DIRTY OIL

2.11   Centrifugal oil cleaner (*Scania*)

units are cooled directly by seawater, although of course there are also air-cooled examples of these. Larger, multi-cylinder engines tend to have freshwater systems with heat exchangers for the main cooling circuit although seawater may be used for oil coolers, turboblower intercoolers and exhaust manifolds. Some of the bigger diesel engines are air-cooled – as the Lister and Deutz – but both of these companies make water cooled units also and a choice is given over most of the power range.

With water cooling thermostat control is usual and it is as important as with the petrol unit that the engine should achieve its operating temperature as quickly as possible since most wear comes about through low temperature running. It should be noted that small engines which have elementary seawater cooling systems can easily be over-cooled so that they never reach their optimum running temperature. In such a case the input of cooling water should never be restricted but experiment with a cock by which the outflow via the exhaust or otherwise might be regulated could be worthwhile.

In the event of overheating the usual checks should be made on the circulation system; first the water outlet, whether via the exhaust or otherwise, to ensure that there is a flow through; then the filter on the

2.12   Bowman heat exchanger with header tank on Thornycroft 90 diesel.
(*Author*)

inlet seacock, the pipe run and the throughput of the seawater pump.
The additional checks on a heat exchanger system are: the header tank
in the freshwater circulating system, the thermostat, and the throughput of the freshwater pump. The thermostat may be checked by temporary removal of the capsule and valve to see if the engine runs at
normal temperature without it.

Exhaust Silencing

Exhaust silencing presents no particular problems with a diesel unit.
But yellow metals and related alloys such as copper, brass or bronze
should never be used anywhere in the system due to the corrosive action

of diesel exhaust gases in conjuction with seawater. Iron and stainless steel are satisfactory. Because of the lower exhaust gas temperature possible vis-à-vis a petrol engine the further reduction in heat which can be achieved with manifold cooling and/or water injection (Fig.2.13) makes it feasible to use synthetic rubber piping and mufflers in the system as the final silencing arrangement. The difference in exhaust temperature which may be gained by improved fuelling is very significant; an engine which is efficient to the extent of having only a small unburnt component in the exhaust gases may have an exhaust manifold temperature low enough for it to be bearable to the hand. An improvement in thermal efficiency of this kind obviously has other benefits, for the environmental conditions of the engine and other equipment in the engine compartment will also have been improved.

The pipe run from the engine to the hull outlet needs the same consideration as given in Chapter 1 for petrol units in regard to fall and water ingress. A diesel on anti-vibration mountings can have a rather rough movement at certain parts of its speed range, besides which the continuing degree of vibration is likely to be higher than that of a petrol engine. It is important, therefore, to give the required flexibility to the pipework where it leaves the engine and also advisable to have a flexible mounting on the first attachment to the hull.

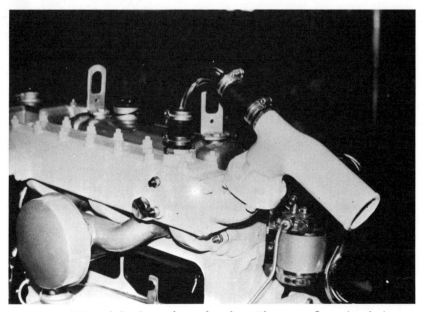

2.13   Water injection exhaust bend on Thornycroft 90. (*Author*)

It is feasible to have a direct underwater discharge from the engine exhaust without intermediate silencing but in that case it would be necessary to ensure that the outlet was at sufficient depth so as never to be exposed by the lift of the hull by the sea. One of the biggest motor yachts built in recent years had the exhaust from its two MAN 1200 bhp diesels arranged in this manner, but that was a larger vessel than most of the engines here would imply.

Starting

Since a diesel has no ancillaries such as carburettor or electrical ignition which could be affected by moisture it will normally start from cold with more certainty than a petrol unit. There is, though, the need to follow an entirely different starting technique; with a spark ignition petrol engine it is inadvisable to continue turning the engine over for more than a few seconds at a time, since if starting is not almost immediate over-choking will occur. With a diesel, the reverse is true since ignition depends on the temperature of the air charge. With a compression ratio of 15:1 or more the charge temperature at the top of the compression stroke will be over 1000°F. On the first few strokes some of this heat will be soaked away by the cold metal of the cylinder and cylinder head but successive compressions will generate more heat until ignition occurs. Thus it may be necessary to engage the starter for a period of 20 seconds or more before the engine responds.

The situation is more likely to make itself apparent with a direct injection engine, for although these have compression ratios high enough to ensure cold starts without starting aids, indirect injection engines are normally fitted with heater plugs which make starting more certain in spite of a lower compression ratio.

If the engine refuses to start after a reasonable amount of turning it is advisable to stop and check around before exhausting the battery. Incidentally, if the engine is being started by hand it is absolutely necessary to keep winding when the decompressor is released; a diesel cannot be taken over top dead centre on compression by a 'pull up' such as serves a petrol unit. Apart from the obvious checks for fuel, etc and the correct throttle setting for starting, the position of the stop control on a multi-cylinder engine should be checked to make sure that it is fully released otherwise no fuel will reach the injectors.

Older engines may have various devices to improve cold starting including auxiliary fuel sprays into the inlet manifold or even provision for putting priming oil directly into the cylinder. It should be noted, though, that if oil is put into the cylinder of a diesel engine the amount must be restricted to a few drops, otherwise, since oil is in-compressible, some damage might be done.

Manifold heaters have also been employed. The CAV Thermostart employs both heat and an auxiliary fuel spray; fitted into the inlet manifold, it has a heater coil powered from the battery and a fuel feed which is sprayed through the hot coil so as to atomize it and make it more readily ignitable in the cold cylinder.

Some of the smaller single and twin cylinder diesels such as are popular for auxiliary use and also larger multi-cylinder engines have a fuel priming button or excess fuel lever which overrides the governor to enable a temporarily larger injection of fuel for starting. The opera-tion is varied; some return to a neutral position automatically after a preset delay, but some need to be reset manually to the neutral position. If the latter is the case it is most important that the lever is returned to the normal running position almost immediately after starting other-wise carboned injectors and a great deal of black smoke will result.

The Sabb diesel has a removable plug into which a chemically treated wad is inserted. The engine will ordinarily start without this aid, but in case of difficulty the plug is removed from the cylinder, charged with a wad and refitted. The wad ignites readily under compression so as to give a start and the residues exit through the exhaust.

Another assistance to cold starting when other means do not produce results is the use of an aerosol of penetrating or rust-inhibiting oil which has some volatile components in it. A short squirt into the air intake can be very effective.

The means of turning the engine over for starting, for the sizes of unit under discussion, will be an electric motor, but other methods such as compressed air and hydraulic starters may be employed, the former particularly on large diesel engines. As with petrol units, whether a separate starter motor or a dynamotor (a combined starter-generator) is fitted depends on the size of the power unit and those other than the small auxiliaries will normally be fitted with a starter motor and a separate generator, which may be either an alternator (AC) or a dynamo (DC).

Electrical Equipment

As indicated, starting a diesel engine from cold can make big demands on electrical storage capacity and in order to obtain the required power with the minimum weight and space being taken up by the batteries it is quite usual for larger engines to have 24V instead of 12V systems, so that the same power is available with only half the current drain. Another aspect of the requirement is the rapidity with which the battery may be recharged to recover its power and in this respect the alternator offers a great advantage over the DC dynamo since its characteristics enable a high charging rate to be achieved at very low rev/min (Fig. 2.14).

The power required to turn an engine over fast against compression may be about 1 hp per litre (1000 cc) of engine capacity, hence, and apart from its limited ability to generate, the dynamotor's restriction to the smaller power units, but some of these may be offered with the optional addition of an alternator to meet the increasing demand for electrical current brought about by modern domestic and navigational aids.

For engines other than small auxiliaries the electrical equipment will be: a dynamo or alternator (the latter with rectifier), an automatic voltage control (AVC), a switch panel with ammeter, and a starter

2.14   Alternator, control unit, fuse box and starter solenoid on Perkins 4.108M engine. (*Author*)

motor with solenoid switch. A manifold fuel spray/heater may be fitted, and indirect injection engines will have igniter plugs in the precombustion chambers plus a tell-tale on the switch panel. A battery is of course needed to complete the circuit but that is not supplied as engine equipment, although the recommended capacity will be given by the engine manufacturer. Operation of the igniter plugs for starting indirect injection engines is normally initiated either by the first part of the movement of the control panel key switch for the starter or a separate heater/starter switch, the second part of the movement which energizes the starter solenoid being delayed until the panel tell-tale indicates that the igniter plugs are at ignition temperature (Fig. 2.15).

There are certain precautions to be observed when an alternator is fitted but it would be sensible to take the same care whatever the generating equipment. Do not disconnect the battery or open the battery master switch while the alternator is in operation. Never reverse the polarity of any connections. Be careful not to cause a short circuit across the alternator terminals. For twin engine installations, twin charging and paralleling of the alternator-battery circuit may be arranged (Fig. 2.16) but dynamos should not be operated in parallel without modification of the control unit to incorporate a balancing winding

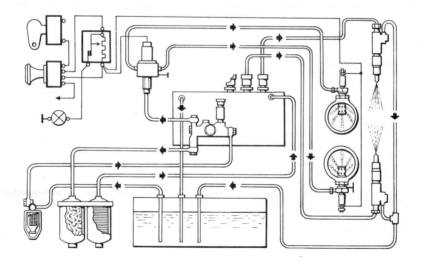

2.15   Fuel system with manifold heater/sprays (flame type) for cold starting (*Deutz*)

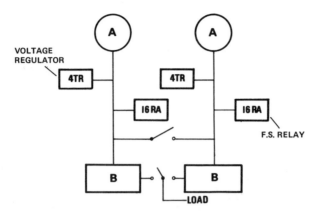

2.16   Twin charging and paralleling of the alternator-battery circuit (*CAV*)

so that in the case of unequal current from the two generators there is no danger of one being damaged through excessive output.

The cutaway drawing of the eight-cylinder in-line Gardner 8LXB shows the general layout and construction of a modern multi-cylinder marine diesel. It develops 176 bhp at 1500 rev/min with a fuel consumption of 0.329 lb/bhp hr (Fig. 2.17).

AUXILIARY AND LAUNCH ENGINES

Petter AB₁WRMR (five-five)   Single cylinder, direct water cooled four-stroke. Mechanical gearbox. 12V electrics with alternator. Max. bhp 5.5 at 3000 rpm. Weight 185 lbs. (Fig. 2.18) *Other models* of 4.7, 9, 18, 25, 37 and 49 bhp.

Yanmar YSE8   Single cylinder, horizontal, water cooled four-stroke. Mechanical gearbox. Electrics optional. Max. bhp 8 at 3200 rpm. Weight 253 lbs. (Fig. 2.19) *Other models* of 12 and 20 bhp.

Bukh DV10M   Single cylinder, water cooled four-stroke with counterbalanced crankshaft. Mechanical gearbox. Electrics optional. Max. bhp 10 at 3000 rpm. Weight 297 lbs. (Fig. 2.20) *Other model*: DV20M 20 bhp.

Volvo Penta MD6A   Two-cylinder, water cooled four-stroke. Mechanical gearbox. Starter/generator. Max. bhp 10 at 2400 rpm.

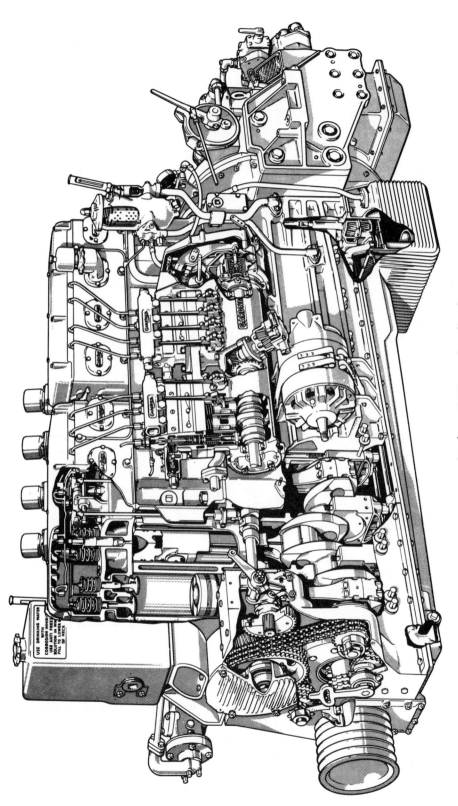

2.17 Gardner 8LXB marine diesel

Weight 355 lbs. (Fig. 2.21) *Other models* (in low power range): MD1B 10 bhp, MD2B 25 bhp, MD3B 36 bhp.

Sabb 2H   Two-cylinder, water cooled four-stroke. V.p. propeller. Electrics optional. Max. bhp 18 at 2250 rpm. Weight 419 lbs. (Fig. 2.22) *Other models*: H 8 bhp, G 10 bhp, GH (air-cooled) 12 bhp, 2G 22 bhp and 2J 30 bhp.

Enfield 85   Single cylinder, air-cooled four-stroke. Manual gearbox. Electrics optional. Max. bhp 7 at 1800 rpm. Weight 330 lbs. *Other models*: 85 (twin cyl.) 14.9 bhp, 100 21 bhp.

Stuart Turner Sole   Single cylinder, direct water cooled four-stroke. Manual gearbox. Siba Dynastart optional. Max. bhp 9 at 2500 rpm. Weight 172 lbs.

Nicor Marine Kittiwake   Single cylinder, air and direct seawater cooled four-stroke. TMP hydraulic gearbox. 12V electrics. Max. bhp 15 at 3000 rpm. Weight 322 lbs..

Farymann P30 M   Two-cylinder (V twin), direct water cooled four-stroke. Mechanical gearbox. Electrics optional. Max. bhp 22 at 2800 rpm. Weight 560 lbs. *Other models*: A30 M 10 bhp, A40 M 10 bhp (hor. engine), R30 M 18 bhp, S30 M 26 bhp.

Lombardini LDAM 672   Two-cylinder, direct water cooled four-stroke. Mechanical gearbox. Electrics optional. Max. bhp 22 at 2800 rpm. Weight 589 lbs. *Other models*: LDAM 450 7 bhp, LDAM 96 10 bhp, LDAM 832 26 bhp, LDAM 833 39 bhp, LDAM 834 52 bhp.

Lister SR3MGR   Three-cylinder, air-cooled four-stroke. Hydraulic gearbox. Electrics optional. Max. bhp 19.5 at 2000 rpm. Weight 710 lbs. (Fig. 2.23) *Other models* (in low power range): SR1M 6.5 bhp, SR2M 13 bhp, ST1M 8.75 bhp, ST2M 17.5 bhp, ST3M 26.25 bhp. Also SW2M (water cooled) 15 bhp.

Renault Couach RC 25 D   Two-cylinder, water cooled four-stroke. Mechanical gearbox. 12V electrics with alternator. Max. bhp 25 at 2200 rpm. Weight 517 lbs. *Other models* in low power range (type no. indicates bhp): RC5D, RC9D, RC11D, RC18D, RC30D.

Watermota Sea Panther   Four-cylinder, HE water cooled four-stroke. Mechanical gearbox. 24V electrics. Max. bhp 30 at 2600 rpm. Weight 385 lbs. (Fig. 2.24).

Kelvin P2   Two-cylinder, water cooled four-stroke. Kelvin manual gearbox. Electrics optional. Max shp 10 at 1500 rpm. Weight 605 lbs. *Other model*: P4 20 shp.

MAIN PROPULSION ENGINES

Wortham Blake Fisherboy 1500   Four-cylinder, HE water cooled four-stroke. HyDrive hydraulic gearbox. Alternator. Max. bhp 36 at 4000 rpm. Weight 490 lbs. (Fig. 2.25)

Brit 154   Four-cylinder, HE water cooled four-stroke. Paragon, Borg-Warner or TMP hydraulic gearbox. 12V electrical equipment. Max. bhp 40 at 2000 rpm. Weight 835 lbs. (Fig. 2.26) *Other model*: Type 281 62 bhp.

Westerbeke Four-107   Four-cylinder, HE water cooled four-stroke. Mechanical Paragon or Hydraulic PRM or Paragon gearbox. 12V electrics. Max. bhp 47 at 4000 rpm. Weight 530 lbs. (Fig. 2.27).

Lister HRW4M   Four-cylinder, HE water cooled four-stroke. Manual or hydraulic gearbox. 12 or 24V electrics. Max. bhp 59 at 2200 rpm. Weight 1400 lbs. (Fig. 2.28) *Other models*: HR2M 29 bhp, HR3M 44 bhp. HR6M 88 bhp, JA6M 138 bhp; all air-cooled. Water cooled units of same power types HRW and JW.

GM 220 M   Four-cylinder, HE water cooled four-stroke. Borg-Warner hydraulic gearbox. 12V electrics. Max. bhp 65 at 2650 rpm. Weight 984 lbs. (Fig. 2.29) *Other models*: 330M 98 bhp, T330M 121 bhp, 466M 146 bhp.

Kelvin R4   Four-cylinder, HE water cooled four-stroke. Kelvin hydraulic gearbox. 24V electrical equipment. Max. shp 75 at 1500 rpm. (Fig. 2.30) *Other models*: R6 112 shp, RS6 150 shp.

RN DM4   Four-cylinder, direct seawater or HE freshwater cooled four-stroke. Electrics optional. Max. bhp 52 at 1500 rpm. Weight 2650 lbs. *Other models*: DM2 26 bhp, DM3 39 bhp, PDM4 48 bhp, EM3

60 bhp, FM3 80 bhp, FM4 107 bhp, EM6 120 bhp, FM5 133 bhp, FM6 160 bhp.

Daf DA475 MkIII   Six-cylinder, HE water cooled four-stroke. Borg-Warner or Twin Disc hydraulic gearbox. Max. bhp 85 at 2500 rpm. Weight 1205 lbs. *Other models*: DD 575 105 bhp, DF 615 118 bhp, DT 615 160 bhp (turbocharged), Dv 825 220 bhp (turbocharged).

MTU MB 6V331 TC 60   Six-cylinder, HE water cooled four-stroke. Max. bhp 430 at 2000 rpm. Weight 3340 lbs. *Other models* of 460, 570, 610, 760, 1150 and 1525 bhp.

Thornycroft 90   Four-cylinder, HE water cooled four-stroke. Borg-Warner, TMP or PRM gearbox. 12V electrics. Max. bhp 38 at 3500 rpm. Weight 665 lbs. *Other models*: 154 62 bhp, 250 80 bhp, 380 120 bhp, T360 150 bhp, T360/1 180 bhp, 760 190 bhp.

Mercedes Benz OM636   Four-cylinder, HE water cooled four-stroke. TMP or Borg-Warner gearbox. 12V electrics. Max. bhp 42 at 3300 rpm. Weight 555 lbs. *Other models*: OM 314 80 bhp, OM 352 125 bhp, OM 346 200 bhp, OM 402 236 bhp, OM 403 295 bhp.

Wizeman WM 54   Four-cylinder, HE water cooled four-stroke. Hydraulic gearbox. 12V electrics. Max. bhp 54 at 3300 rpm. *Other models*: WM 240 240 bhp, WM 300 300 bhp.

Parsons Porbeagle MkII   Four-cylinder, HE water cooled four-stroke. Parsons manual or hydraulic gearbox. 12V electrics. Max. shp 80 at 2500 rpm. Weight 1110 lbs. (Fig. 2.31) *Other models*: Pike MkII 80 shp, Barracuda MkII 120 shp, Force 12 175 shp.

Scania D5   Four-cylinder, HE water cooled four-stroke. Hydraulic gearbox and v.p. propellers as required. Max. bhp 96 at 2000 rpm. Weight 1323 lbs. (Fig. 2.32) *Other models*: D8 142 bhp, D11 181 bhp, DS11 252 bhp, DS5 111 bhp, DS8 173 bhp, Ds11 225 bhp, DSI 14 347 bhp. All DS engines are turbocharged.

Chrysler Nissan M6-33   Six-cylinder, HE water cooled four-stroke. Paragon or Borg-Warner hydraulic gearbox. 12V electrics. Max. shp 100 at 4000 rpm. Weight 824 lbs. *Other model*: M4-33 70 shp.

Renault Couach RC 120D   Six-cylinder, HE water cooled four-stroke. Twin Disc hydraulic gearbox. 12V electrics. Max. bhp 120 at 2500 rpm. Weight 1485 lbs. *Other models*: (type no. indicates bhp) RC45D, RC55D, RC80D, RC100D, RC140D, RC210DT, RC260DV, RC320DV, RC430DV.

Gardner 6LX   Six-cylinder, HE water cooled four-stroke. Twin Disc hydraulic gearbox. 24V electrical equipment. Max. bhp 127 at 1500 rpm. Weight 2796 lbs. (Fig. 2.33) *Other models*: 8L3B 260 bhp, 8LXB 176 bhp.

Perkins T6.354   Six-cylinder turbocharged, HE water cooled four-stroke. Borg-Warner hydraulic gearbox. 24V electrics. Max. shp 145 at 2400 , rpm. Weight 1450 lbs. (Fig. 2.34) *Other models*: P3152 33 shp, 4.108 47 bhp, 4.236 72 shp, 6.354 115 shp, H6.354 115 shp (hor. engine), HT6.354 175 shp, V8.510 160 shp, TV8.510 235 shp.

Foden FD6   Six-cylinder, HE water cooled two-stroke. Foden hydraulic gearbox. 24V electrics. Max. shp 147 at 2000 rpm. Weight 1910 lbs. *Other models*: FD4 100 shp, FD6 MkVII 213 shp, FD12 MkVI 300 shp, FD12 MkVII 427 shp.

Tempest 6/180   Six-cylinder turbocharged, HE water cooled four-stroke. Borg-Warner or Self Changing Gears gearbox. 24V electrics. Max. bhp 180 at 2450 rpm. Weight 1430 lbs. (Fig. 2.35) *Other models*: Tempest/Leyland (BLMC ex-BMC): Captain 31 bhp, Commander 50 bhp, Commodore 62 bhp, Sea Lord 96 bhp (all continuous bhp). Tempest/Ford: 4/58 58 bhp, 4/80 80 bhp, 6/120 120 bhp, 6/150 150 bhp, 6/250 turbocharged 250 bhp.

Caterpillar 3160   V-8 cylinder, HE water cooled four-stroke. Twin Disc hydraulic gearbox. 12V electrics. Max. bhp 210 at 2800 rpm. Weight 1640 lbs. (Fig. 2.36) *Other models*: D330T 200 bhp, D333T 300 bhp, D334TA 360 bhp, D343TA 550 bhp, D346TA 730 bhp, D348TA 1100 bhp, and others up to 1700 bhp.

Rolls-Royce C6M 210   Six-cylinder, HE water cooled four-stroke. Twin Disc hydraulic gearbox. 24V electrics. Max. bhp 210 at 2100 rpm. Weight 3310 lbs. *Other models*: C6M 265 265 bhp, C6M 310 310 bhp, C8M 410 410 bhp, DV8NM 470 bhp, DV8TM 565 bhp, DV8TCWM 750 bhp.

Deutz F8L 413   V-8 cylinder, air-cooled four-stroke. Hydraulic gearbox and v.p. propellers. Electric or air starting. Max. bhp 217 at 2650 rpm. Weight 1620 lbs. *Other models*: A large range of uni-directional, air and water cooled engines comprising 32 types from 14 up to 1140 bhp is available.

Cummins V555M   V-8 cylinder, HE water cooled four-stroke, Borg-Warner, Twin Disc and Capitol gearboxes. 24V electrics. Max. bhp 240 at 3300 rpm. Weight 2020 lbs. (Fig. 2.37) *Other models*: V-504-M 210 bhp, VT8-370M 370 bhp, V-903M 320 bhp, VT-903-M 400 bhp, NH-250-M 250 bhp, NT-335-M bhp, NT-380-M 380 bhp, V12-500-M 500 bhp, VT12-635-M 635 bhp, VT12-700-M 700 bhp, VT12-800-M 800 bhp.

Volvo Penta TAMD 120A   Six-cylinder turbocharged, HE water cooled four-stroke. Twin Disc or Borg-Warner gearbox. 24V electrics. Max. bhp 356 at 2200 rpm. Weight 4035 lbs. (Fig. 2.38) *Other models*: MD 21A 75 bhp, MD 32A 106 bhp, TMD 70B 200 bhp, TAMD 70B 250 bhp, THAMD 70B 250 bhp, TMD 120A 320 bhp.

GM Detroit Diesel 12V-71   V-12 cylinder, HE water cooled two-stroke. Twin Disc hydraulic gearbox. 24V electrics. Max. bhp 525 at 2300 rpm. Weight 4925 lbs. (Fig. 2.39) *Other models*: 4-53 140 bhp, 4-71 175 bhp, 6V-53 216 bhp, 6-71 265 bhp, 6-71 M 280 bhp, 6V-71 265 bhp, 8V-71 350 bhp, 8V-71TI 435 bhp, 12V-71TI 675 bhp, 16V-71 700 bhp, 12V-149 800 bhp, 16V-149 1060 bhp.

COMPANIES MARINIZING FORD ENGINES (UK)

C-Power Industries Ltd
Mermaid Marine Engines Ltd
Tempest Diesels Ltd
Powermarine Engines Ltd
Transport Equipment (Thornycroft) Ltd
Watermota Ltd
Wortham Blake & Co. Ltd
Sabre Marine Ltd
Parsons Engineering Co. Ltd
Delta Marine Engineers Ltd
REFA Ltd

2.18   Petter AB1WRMR

2.19   Yanmar YSE8

2.20   Bukh DV10M

2.21   Volvo Penta MD6A

2.22   Sabb 2H

2.23   Lister SR3MGR

2.24   Watermota Sea Panther

2.25   Wortham Blake Fisherboy 1500

2.26   Brit 154

2.27   Westerbeke Four-107

2.28   Lister HRW4MGR

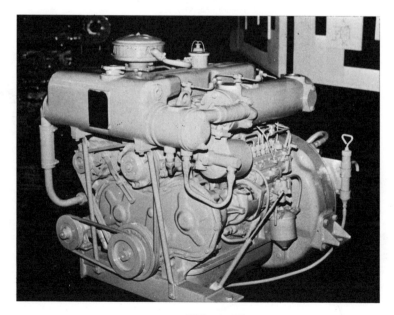

2.29   GM 220 M

2.30   Kelvin R4

2.31   Parsons Porbeagle

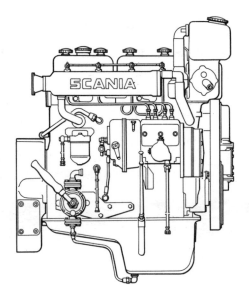

2.32   Scania D5

2.33   Gardner 6LX

2.34   Perkins T6.354

2.35   Tempest 6/180

2.36   Caterpillar 3160

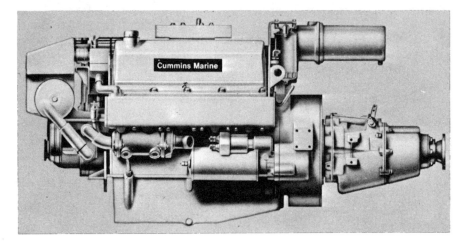

2.37   Cummins V555M

2.38　Volvo Penta TAMD 120A

2.39　GM 12V-71

3. Rotary Engines

The idea of an internal combustion engine working on a conventional cycle but without reciprocating parts was realized as a technical proposition by Dr Felix Wankel some years ago, but it has taken the attention of development teams in Europe, the USA and Japan to bring the unit to a stage where reliability allied to performance could make it competitive with the reciprocating IC engine. As far as performance is concerned there has never been much doubt about what the rotary engine could offer in terms of high power with minimum weight and size, but the outstanding question mark for a long time was its longevity, chiefly concerning the life of the rotor gas seals, and fuel consumption. Research has now indicated the material and the method by which these tip seals can operate satisfactorily and with an acceptable life under varying speeds and loads; but fuel economy has yet to be mastered to the extent that it is at all times competitive with a conventional IC unit.

To give a brief description of the Wankel as a single rotor unit (Fig. 3.1). The trochoid housing, which has the shape of two intersecting circles, provides a chamber which in conjunction with the orbiting rotor has the necessary variable volume when swept by rotary movement. The rotor both follows the movement of the crankshaft, being mounted on its cam-type throw, and also rotates about the throw. The apex or tip seals of the three-sided rotor faces are always in contact with the rotor housing, thus the three rotor faces are isolated from each other and each face makes a separate combustion chamber.

The required sequence of events – induction, compression, power stroke (segment) and exhaust – can all be achieved by each of the faces in one revolution of the rotor as they successively uncover the inlet port, sparkplug and exhaust port in the trochoid housing.

The speed of rotation of the rotor about the crankshaft throw is timed to the crankshaft by an internal ring gear in the rotor body

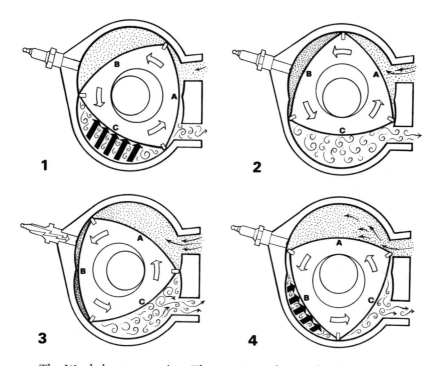

3.1   The Wankel rotary engine. The sequence shows what happens in one-third of a revolution of the rotor. *1*   Face A has uncovered the inlet port and is starting its induction phase; B is compressing its fuel/air charge; at C the charge has been ignited and the face is on its power phase. *2*   A continues induction; B is nearing end of compression phase; C has uncovered exhaust port and is discharging spent gases. *3*   A is continuing induction; at B charge is fully compressed and being ignited; C is continuing exhaust phase. *4*   A is closing inlet port to start compression; B is in power phase; C is nearing end of exhaust phase. Thus in one complete revolution of the rotor all three faces will have completed their power cycle.

which engages with a stationary pinion locked to the housing side face. This pinion is concentric with the crankshaft main journals and provides a bearing for the shaft at one end. The ratio is such that for each complete revolution of the crankshaft the rotor will make one-third of a turn and one face of the rotor will have moved through only a third of its combustion sequence, but because the rotor has three faces there will be three power pulses for each complete rotation, i.e. one for each revolution of the crankshaft, which as indicated is turning at three times the speed of rotation of the rotor. In doing this it will be observed that the engine is giving the same number of power pulses per revolution of the crankshaft as a conventional single cylinder reciprocating two-stroke motor, but the Wankel accomplishes this while operating on the Otto four-phase cycle.

Although the combined effect of the two rotary movements – the rotor turning with the crank throw and turning about it simultaneously – while following the shape of the housing causes the outline of the rotor to orbit and its mass to make a circular path, the out of balance forces do not appear to be very significant and since it is possible to 'stack up' the units an engine of two or four units can be balanced by opposing the crankshaft throws (Fig. 3.2).

The single rotor engine was developed by OMC for use in snowmobiles and the work covered the requirement for a lightweight trouble-free unit so successfully that progression to the Johnson multiple rotor water cooled outboard engine was greatly advanced by the knowledge gained. The snowmobile engine is air-cooled and lubrication is by a petroil mixture of 50:1 as employed in the conventional two-stroke outboard engine. Further cooling is provided by taking the incoming fuel/air charge through the centre of the rotor before it is introduced into the rotor housing. This system of charge cooling lowers the volumetric efficiency of the engine somewhat because the charge is heated as it passes through the rotor and it also picks up heat from the air-cooled casing, but it was chosen as an acceptable alternative to the additional complexities of oil cooling. For marine use the employment of water instead of air for cooling the casing brings an improvement in efficiency.

There are charge air intake ports in both the side and the periphery of the rotor housing so that the stable low speed running given by side porting can be augmented by the better volumetric efficiency of the radial port at speed.

Ignition is by a CD system which enables the use of a surface gap sparkplug so as to give the minimum break in the continuity of the casing inner surface against which the rotor tip seals bear. The tip seals are in two pieces to compensate for expansion of the rotor housing with the minimum leakage.

Due to the Wankel engine geometry the sparkplug is never cooled by the incoming charge to the same extent as it is in a conventional reciprocating engine and consequently it has to withstand continuing high temperature. Another hot area is at the exhaust port, since this never closes and very hot gases are concentrated there from the triple

3.2   OMC Johnson four-rotor outboard engine (the lowest unit is hidden by the casing). (*Author*)

combustion which is taking place with every revolution of the rotor: thus there can be a cooling as well as a silencing problem in the exhaust arrangements – the rotary engine is very sensitive to back-pressure. But both of these difficulties may be more easily dealt with in a marine application.

In construction, the OMC rotary incorporates some tried materials from that company's long experience with high performance outboard engines. Aluminium alloy as specified for the reciprocating engine pistons is used for the rotor housing, but to minimize wear from the tool steel rotor tip seals which bear on this the inside of the housing is sprayed with tungsten carbide and this hard deposit is then ground and honed. The side housings are hypereutectic silicon aluminium alloy, lapped to a good surface but not otherwise treated.

With the requirement for an integral gear ring in the rotor the material for that component needed to have impact strength as well as good physical properties under thermal stress; pearlitic nodular cast iron was chosen as best meeting the specification. The rotor is carried on a large roller bearing running on the crankshaft cam throw and the crankshaft itself runs in needle rollers which save both space and cost (Fig. 3.3).

Some of the advantages of the Wankel engine are that it has fewer moving parts, it is very compact, it can give high power using low-

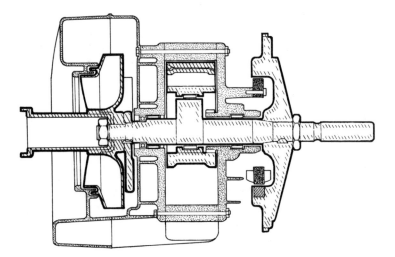

3.3 Cross-section of single rotor unit, parallel to crankshaft (*OMC*)

octane, non-leaded petrol, and it has a high power/weight ratio which may be in order of 2 lbs per brake horsepower. Currently, although there are now many standard units operating satisfactorily in automobiles, there is no production model available generally for marine use, but examples have been raced and exhibited for this purpose. It is probable that the first standard engines produced in quantity for marine use will be outboard units, since as indicated the engine as developed by OMC may be either air or water cooled and they have already made a number of both types.

With regard to power output and fuel consumption, the Wankel will give a much higher output from a given engine capacity but the fuel consumption is heavier than that of a reciprocating engine developing comparable power, e.g. the OMC snowmobile unit discussed develops 35 bhp at 5500 rpm from 528 cc but with a fuel consumption of 0.73 lbs/bhp hr. As an approximate comparison, a reciprocating engine example offers 35 bhp at 3500 rpm from 1100 cc with a fuel consumption of 0.43 lbs/bhp hr.

There seems to be no reason why the Wankel engine should not be used with any of the available means of transmission. Many existing multi-cylinder petrol units operate at maximum speeds similar to that of the rotary example, but in view of the rotary's rev/min capabilities some applications in conjunction with conventional sterngear would call for considerable reduction gearing. Water jet units, some of which are able to operate at high speeds without loss of efficiency, could make an attractive combination since they would be suited to the higher rev/min of the Wankel without intermediate gearing.

Another promising but not so immediate prospect in the rotary engine field is the considerable research and development which has been undertaken to produce a gas turbine suitable for trucks and buses. It is believed that one manufacturer has reached a very advanced stage in the development of a viable unit, but for the time being the details are not available. Remembering that the road vehicle diesel already provides the basic unit for so many boat installations it may be conjectured that a gas turbine designed to meet road vehicle requirements might also be very well suited for marine applications. A fuel economy suitable for road haulage would be acceptable to the owner of a motor vessel, and the other aspects of performance would no doubt be at least comparable with present power units, besides having perhaps a greater flexibility in the kind of fuel which they may use.

As a powerful means of propulsion without great reference to fuel economy the gas turbine has been in use in Royal Navy ships for a number of years, both for light patrol craft and in larger vessels as an additional means of power for emergency speed. It has also been installed in racing power boats and the offshore power racer *Miss Embassy* is a good example. She is fitted with a Rolls-Royce Gnome engine modified by the Gas Turbine Division of Hovercraft Ltd (Fig. 3.4). This unit develops 1050 bhp with a cruising power of 900 bhp and has an all-up weight of 360 lbs – a power/weight ratio of 0.34 lbs/hp. But it uses 75 gal of fuel per hour. However, if these figures are analysed it is seen that what looks like an astronomical fuel consumption is actually 0.82 lbs/bhp hr – which is still rather more than most owners would care to finance, but does not seem excessive for the type of unit.

However, the kerosene fuel which the turbine uses, although no longer cheap is still much less expensive than petrol and it might be that the required tankage and its weight would be more of a handicap than its cost, supposing that the above consumption is taken as representative per bhp hr for a smaller production engine such as would be suitable for fast dayboats and express cruisers.

No doubt there will be continuing development in this field; reliability does not seem to be in doubt for it is claimed that the Gnome engine as modified by Hovercraft Ltd will run for 2000 hours between overhauls.

3.4   Rolls-Royce Gnome 1050 bhp gas turbine. Hovercraft Ltd. (*Eric Coltham*)

4. Outboard Engines

There are many examples of both two and four stroke outboard engines and OMC have produced a four-cycle rotary unit which could influence the trend in high performance motors of the future, but beyond this current outboards whether large or small in power output are predominantly two-stroke reciprocating engines. The development of the two-cycle engine in this particular field has probably gone further than that in any other.

Of the larger units, the USA, Sweden and Japan as manufacturers share most of the market for these as well as making a range of smaller models. To deal first with the outboards made in Britain, these are mostly of suitable power for tenders, small workboats and auxiliary use in small sailing vessels. They range from approximately 1 to 6 hp and some of the best known, such as the Seagull, are very basic and rugged in design and construction with a single cylinder power head employed over the whole range. Simplicity is the keynote for this and other low power, UK manufactured units; the carburettor is most often a Bowden cable controlled variable single jet, and cross-flow scavenging is usual, with the exhaust taken below water. Both water and air cooled engines are available in the low power range. Usually there is no astern gear or neutral position where the propeller is disengaged, but some have a clutch and with many it is possible to get power astern by rotating the whole unit through 180°. Most of these small units have integral fuel tanks and little attempt is made to style or streamline the package, but in spite of the general lack of concern for appearance they do the job and some have a notable longevity—frequently under treatment which would destroy most machinery.

In common with inboard two-stroke engines, these also are subject to occasional starting difficulty through condensation or oil fouling the plugs, or both. The flywheel magneto which is standard on these units may sometimes become rather feeble through the insulation of the field coils having existed too long in either damp or oily conditions; the former will depend upon where the unit is kept when out of use, but the latter may not be so easily recognized as a contribution to poor starting when the unit has had considerable wear. Oil blow-by from the crankcase has direct access to the underside of the flywheel where the coils and contact breaker are housed and fouling of the contact breaker points will weaken or even prevent a spark at the plug. The effect tends to be cumulative for if the spark is too poor to permit starting with the first few pulls the excess unignited fuel mixture will probably foul the plug sufficiently to prevent starting with further attempts. In view of this it is advisable not to persist; a quicker start will be made by cleaning the plug and if possible draining the crankcase.

It may not be generally recognized that a significant concentration of oil can build up in the crankcase of a two-stroke engine when it is running slowly, through condensation of oil from the petrol/oil mixture, and it does not wholly disperse with faster running. Engines using a 50:1 mixture have been found to have an oil concentration of as much as 30% in the drainings from the crankcase. This represents a fuel mix of about $3\frac{1}{2}$:1 and the probable difficulty of starting when some of this is added to the incoming fuel/air charge is apparent. It may be wrong to assume that engines which run on lower petrol/oil ratios are prone to even higher residual oil concentrations but it is reasonable to suppose that they suffer to some degree from the same effect. For some years now the larger, multi-cylinder outboard engines have been designed to re-cycle the crankcase condensate so that they are in effect self-draining.

Small engines which normally run on a fairly oil-rich mixture are not notably fussy as to the exact proportions of the mix for starting, but if the engine has been out of use for some time or is consistently difficult to start it may be advisable to drain the crankcase and also the carburettor and the fuel tank since the more volatile elements of the fuel mix might have dispersed. This suggestion re carburettor and fuel tank applies of course to engines of any size or date if they have been out of use for a long time.

Occasional inspection of the contact breaker points is advisable to ensure easier starting and reliable running. Assuming that they are correctly gapped, their cleanliness is easily proven by drawing a small piece of clean card between them. Contact breaker gap setting is critical to performance so an attempt should be made to get it absolutely right according to the maker's recommendation. Put just a smear of grease on the crankshaft cam so that the fibre pad does not wear rapidly and thus alter the setting.

There are several four-stroke outboard engines available up to about 8 hp, and a 55 hp model is produced in the USA. Somewhat better fuel economy may be expected from a four-stroke unit, and perhaps better and more even pulling power at low speed, but to date such advantages as they have do not appear to have caused them to displace the two-stroke in popularity. In regard to fuel consumption, the economy of these smaller engines whether two or four stroke is rarely closely examined, but a two-stroke unit may use about the same quantity of fuel per bhp/hr as the Gnome gas turbine discussed in the previous chapter. It is of little significance in the case of a 5 hp engine but large units of 50, 100 or even 150 bhp can make their thirst very apparent.

In recent years the greatly increased market for small power craft such as water ski boats and midget weekend cruisers has meant a similar uplift in the sales of portable power units of a size sufficient to give a brisk planing performance. As indicated, the demand for outboard engines of this capacity is met wholly from outside the UK, but the requirement is established to the extent that full sales and service facilities are widely available. Smaller units from the same sources are also offered in a comprehensive range from 2 hp up, and many of these have some of the refinements incorporated in their larger brothers; e.g. twin cylinders, and forward, neutral and reverse gears, etc.

The Johnson 50 hp unit provides a good example of what may be expected of a modern outboard engine in the middle power range. This is a two-cylinder, two-stroke motor with loop scavenging and CD (capacitor discharge) ignition. Efficient breathing is ensured with twin carburettors and the exhaust is tuned, water cooled and discharged below water (Fig. 4.1). Both starting and gear change may be either manual or electric. The engine develops 50 bhp at 5500 rpm; the standard propeller is three-bladed, $13\frac{1}{4}$ in dia $\times$ 15 in pitch, and the overall gear ratio is 12.32:1. The crankshaft on the engine is supported by three main bearings, two roller and one ball type; roller bearings are also used for the connecting rod big ends. The pistons are only slightly domed and the piston skirts are ported to accommodate the loop scavenging system. Intakes from the carburettors to the crankcase are fitted with leaf valves which open as the crankcase pressure drops. The fuel pump also operates on pressure difference in the crankcase. The fixed jet carburettors have high and low speed jets, the latter being adjustable for slow speed running (Fig. 4.2). The choke may be manually or electrically operated.

Principal components of the CD ignition system are shown in Fig.

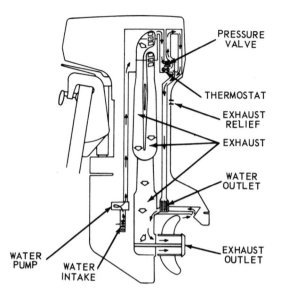

4.1   Cooling and exhaust systems, Johnson 50 hp outboard

4.3. Briefly, the operation is as follows. Two charge coils are mounted on the alternator stator which is located under the flywheel. The flywheel-mounted magnets which induce current in the alternator stator also generate some 300V AC in the charge coils as the flywheel rotates. This current is converted to DC in the power pack and stored in the power pack capacitor.

Also situated under the flywheel is a sensor coil which reacts to a sensor magnet integral with the flywheel hub; the magnet has two gaps which time the impulse from the sensor coil. The small voltage generated in the sensor coil activates the electronic switches in the power pack; each of these switches is able to discharge the 300 V stored in the capacitor into one of the ignition coils, there being an ignition coil for each spark plug. The coil steps up the voltage so that it is about 30,000 V when fed to the plug. After discharge the electronic switch opens and the charge coils recharge the capacitor. The second sensor magnet gap, opposite in polarity from the first, generates a reverse polarity voltage in the sensor coil and this activates the second electronic switch in the power pack and causes the capacitor to discharge

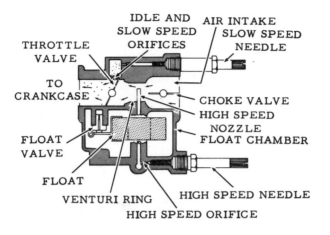

4.2   Carburettor, Johnson 50 hp

into the other ignition coil. The process is then repeated. A surface gap spark plug is used which gives a large electrode area with a consistent gap and the high voltage tends to make the plug self-cleaning.

Most outboard engine manufacturers now fit CD ignition on the large units and there are other developments in common use such as the 'thru-the-hub' exhaust where the gases are discharged through the centre of the propeller. Scavenge systems still vary on the larger engines producing comparable power; Johnson, Evinrude and Archimedes Penta are loop scavenged while Mercury and Chrysler have cross flow systems, the former in conjunction with a ported piston (Figs 4.4, 4.5, 4.6).

The conventional outboard engine bottom end drive is by bevel gears and those engines with a gearshift for forward, neutral and reverse have two facing bevel wheels with which the drive shaft pinion is always engaged. The bevel wheels are mounted on the propeller shaft but are only engaged to drive via a dog clutch which is splined to the shaft. Fore-and-aft movement of the clutch causes it to engage with either the forward or reverse bevel gear, with an intermediate position where it is free of both (neutral). The arrangement is common to all outboards with a forward-neutral-reverse (FNR) gearshift. Fig. 4.7 shows how the gear change on the Johnson 50 is operated when an electric gearshift is incorporated. The additional components are an oil pump to power the movement of the dog clutch and two solenoids

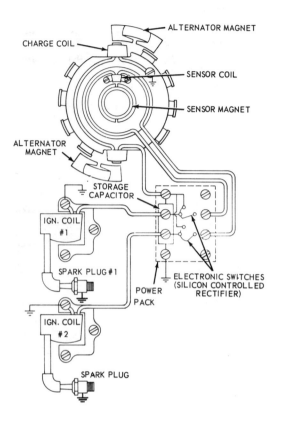

CHARGE COIL

ALTERNATOR MAGNET

SENSOR COIL

SENSOR MAGNET

ALTERNATOR
MAGNET

STORAGE
CAPACITOR

IGN. COIL
#1

SPARK PLUG #1

POWER
PACK

ELECTRONIC SWITCHES
(SILICON CONTROLLED
RECTIFIER)

IGN. COIL
#2

SPARK PLUG

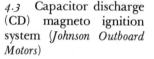

4.3 Capacitor discharge (CD) magneto ignition system *(Johnson Outboard Motors)*

which operate the ball valves controlling the flow of oil from the pump to the shift piston.

All but the smallest outboard can now be provided with generating equipment, and an increasing range of remote controls facilitated by electrical operation is now available for the large units; starting, choke movement, gearshift and power trim can now all be operated from a remote helm position. Some of these, e.g. the choke and starter switch, can be operated directly by a solenoid, which is a simple coil winding round a core which moves longitudinally when current flows through the coil; for movements requiring more power the operation is electro-hydraulic with the solenoid controlling an oil valve – as the gearshift mechanism in Fig. 4.7. The working of a solenoid for choke operation is generally in conjunction with a thermal switch on the engine exhaust

4.4 Archimedes Penta 600 loop scavenged, CD ignition 60 bhp engine. (*Author*)

which opens at a predetermined temperature and cuts the current to the solenoid, thus causing the choke to be released.

Engine cooling may also be monitored electrically with a heat switch triggering a warning buzzer should the cylinder head temperature rise abnormally. On many small outboard engines the safeguard is a visible discharge of cooling water after it has been circulated, but this is not feasible where the coolant is discharged below water and some part of it may also be used to cool and contract the exhaust gases.

Water temperature on the larger engines is also thermostatically controlled and the system is much the same as with a direct sea-water cooled inboard engine, using an eccentric vane pump with a flexible rotor. At low speed the impeller works as a displacement pump with the blades in contact with the housing; at higher speeds the resistance of the water deflects the blades and the pump action is centrifugal (Fig. 4.8).

4.5   Mercury 150 bhp six-cylinder, six-carburettor power head. (*Author*)

4.6 Chrysler 60 two-cylinder power head with Magnapower CD ignition. (*Author*)

Correct trim angle is important for all outboards and especially so for the more powerful units. Manual adjustment is incorporated on all engines, but fast craft fitted with high power motors can benefit from an adjustment which is available to the driver while the boat is at speed. Operation is typically electro-hydraulic, and in the Chrysler system an electric pump controlled from the helm position actuates a hydraulic ram. A position indicator tells the driver at what angle of trim, bow up or down, the boat is running (Fig. 4.9).

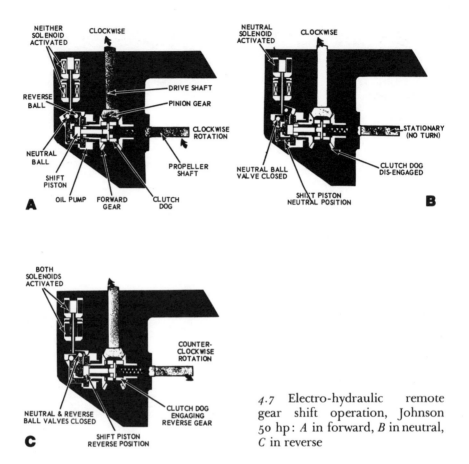

4.7 Electro-hydraulic remote gear shift operation, Johnson 50 hp: *A* in forward, *B* in neutral, *C* in reverse

4.8 Water impeller action: left, at low speed; right, at high speed (*Johnson*)

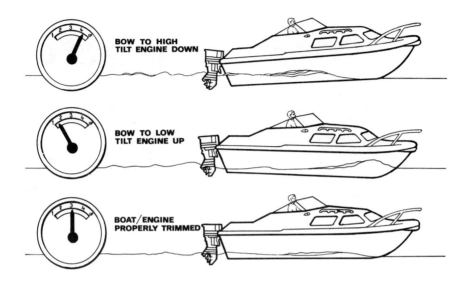

4.9   Trimming effect: dashboard indicator gives trim angle. Chrysler power trim

5. Engine Conversions

Both petrol and diesel engines can be marinized satisfactorily; the marinization of a suitable diesel from a truck is just as feasible as a similar job on a petrol unit but the transmission will need to be more robust. For those who do not want to do the job themselves there are many firms specializing in this work, all of whom would supply a marinized unit, and some of them will also convert a customer's engine. Enthusiasts who wish to work on their own engines will find that the situation is eased considerably by the number of manufacturers who now supply the components for conversion of popular standard road vehicle engines. Complete marinization kits are now available (Fig. 5.1) and with one of these an owner is able to complete a unit to professional standards.

Besides fitting the engine with suitable cooling and exhaust arrangements there is the basic question of transmission, and perhaps this should be considered first because the type of engine will to some extent indicate the transmission system.

Diesel engines which are not likely to operate at such high rev/min as petrol units are very suitable for conventional sterngear with a mechanical or hydraulic gear box, whereas with a petrol engine the scope is widened since other means of propulsion such as outdrives and water jets become more practicable. Of course both of these, and hydraulic drives, may also be employed with a diesel engine, but outdrives and water jets particularly can be very compatible with a petrol motor. A water jet impeller is able to operate efficiently at much higher rpm than a conventional propeller and consequently a direct drive without intermediate gearing becomes possible; further, the astern provision is incorporated in the jet unit so another requirement is met. Finally, installation is somewhat more simple since there is no lining up of sterngear or any special provision for taking thrust, which is also taken care of in the jet unit.

5.1   Marinization kit for Ford 1600, Lancing Marine. (*Eric Coltham*)

With regard to thrust, it should be noted that all marine gear-boxes and drives have bearings incorporated to take the thrust from the propeller, but a car or truck gearbox is not designed to cope with end thrust; therefore if it is for any reason incorporated in the installation it must be protected by a separate thrust bearing in the transmission line (Figs. 5.2, 5.3).

The means of transmission, whether conventional marine gearbox or not, will probably be the most expensive part of the conversion and this is another reason for considering the possibilities in close relation to your intended power unit. At a time when prices are continually changing it is not possible to be very factual about comparable costs of installations but taking a multi-cylinder petrol engine of up to about 45 bhp as an example, the relative cost situation indicated is that the least expensive transmission would be either a mechanical gearbox with conventional sterngear or a water jet unit. A hydraulic gearbox with sterngear would cost rather more, and an inboard/outboard drive would perhaps also be more expensive. The relative cost situation changes somewhat when considering larger power units, and also the type of hull and its configuration will have a great deal to do with the final choice: it is possible to think of examples where the sterndrive,

5.2   Thrust bearing which also steadies the shaft (*Gaines*)

although apparently expensive for low to medium power units, would provide the most likely answer.

As the power increases the means of transmission may change their order in the cost table; a water jet unit to transmit more than about 50 hp will probably cost as much, if not more, than a conventional transmission or sterndrive. It is sensible therefore for the potential marinizer not to be influenced by the cost of other installations but to obtain specific quotations for his own requirement for the different methods of transmission to which he believes his boat to be suited, and unless he has some knowledge in the matter it will be wise to obtain a professional opinion as to what might serve best.

5.3   Flexible shaft coupling which will also take thrust (*Gaines*)

The work involved in converting a power unit to marine use is not extensive and the number of new components required is comparatively few. This is a typical list (as used by Lancing Marine for conversion of the Ford 1600 GT car engine).

Water cooled exhaust manifold
Cylinder head water outlet fitting
Water pump with pressure warning switch
Oil cooler and filter
Skin fitting for water inlet (a seacock and filter could be substituted for this)
Tachometer
Starter motor mounting
Starter motor solenoid switch
Flywheel adapter and coupling for transmission
Ignition solenoid
Warning lights for ignition and oil and water pressure
Engine mounting frame. (The nature of this depends upon the engine type and the kind of transmission to which it will be coupled. The frame in Fig. 5.1 is suitable for a sterndrive. For conventional transmission no frame may be required.)

In conversion the gearbox and bell housing and the original exhaust manifold are removed, also the water pump; the rest of the major engine components are retained. A new starter motor mounting will not be necessary for some installations; it is included in the above list because the particular type of engine mounting requires it. The water pump and generator will normally be belt-driven as before, but in some instances it will be necessary to fit a new fanbelt to accommodate a different diameter of V pulley on the water pump.

Since a boat engine is likely to be run at a constant speed over quite long periods and the power output of an internal combustion engine depends upon the rev/min, it is necessary to decide at what speed the marinized unit will run when installed in the boat with its appropriate gearing, if any. The principal considerations are the desired performance, the size and shape of the boat, and the power needed to reconcile these. But road vehicle engines do not flourish from being run continuously at full power, and therefore if it is intended to use an engine of which only the maximum power and rev/min are known it is necessary to calculate what power may be expected at lower rev/min such as would be suitable for continuous operation.

The following formula will give the approximate horsepower of a four-stroke petrol engine at the chosen rev/min:

$$hp = \frac{B \times B \times S \times C \times rev/min}{13,440}$$

For a two-stroke:

$$hp = \frac{B \times B \times S \times C \times rev/min}{8400}$$

For a four-stroke high speed diesel engine:

$$hp = \frac{B \times B \times S \times C \times rev/min}{11,800}$$

B = cylinder bore in inches
S = stroke in inches
C = the number of cylinders

The following notes with regard to the power requirement for different hulls are of course equally applicable to other power units as well as conversions, but it is convenient to give an outline of the considerations here since the potential marinizer, unless he is professionally advised, will need to make a reasonable assessment himself. It is recommended that if there is any doubt as to the suitability of an intended installation professional advice should be sought since a major error could be expensive as well as disappointing.

In the case of a displacement boat it is taken that the optimum speed is related to the waterline length and it may be found with this formula:

$$V = K \times \sqrt{WL}$$

V = speed in knots
K = speed/length ratio
WL = waterline length in feet

The speed/length ratio K will vary according to the type of hull but it is considered that an average figure for a boat without any flat sections aft, that is a double ended or canoe stern, or narrow transom hull, will be about 1.33. If the hull has more lift aft, such as might be given by flatter sections or a broader transom at the waterline, the figure of 1.33 may be improved upon, but it is an average which will be applicable to a variety of displacement hulls.

Thus, using the above formula; the example being 25 ft on the waterline:

$$V = 1.33 \times \sqrt{25} \qquad \text{which is } 1.33 \times 5 = 6.65 \text{ knots}$$

This is the speed up to which the boat may be driven easily and economically and above which increases in power will not bring proportionate improvement in performance. Fig. 5.4 applies to both displacement and planing boats and gives an indication of the power requirement for a typical example of each. From the curve for the displacement boat it will be seen that the power applied to drive the boat beyond its optimum speed gives sharply diminishing returns. The curve for the planing boat indicates that it requires more power than a displacement vessel for the speed up to which it begins to plane, and thereafter, having got over the hump, the power needed actually diminishes slightly for a period although the speed of the boat is increasing.

Assuming that the transmission and the propeller give reasonable standards of efficiency (see note below), the following formula will give an approximate indication of the power required to drive different types of planing hulls at a given speed, and the speed which may be obtained from a given power:

$$\text{bhp} = \text{Displacement (tons)} \times \left[\frac{\text{Speed (knots)}}{\text{K}} \right]^2$$

or

$$\text{Speed (knots)} = \text{K} \times \sqrt{\frac{\text{bhp}}{\text{Displacement (tons)}}}$$

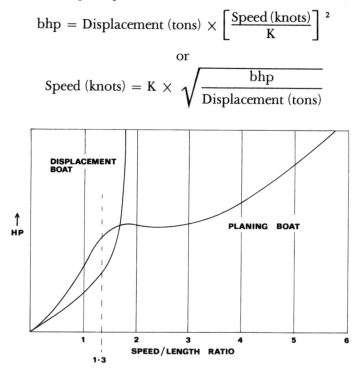

5.4   Power – speed/length ratio (*courtesy Perkins Engines Ltd*)

Values for K are given in the table:

Waterline length (feet)	16	20	25	30	40	50
Shallow V hulls	2.8	3.0	3.25	3.48	3.95	4.40
Medium V hulls	2.5	2.65	2.90	3.15	3.60	4.10
Deep Hulls	2.35	2.55	2.75	3.0	3.50	3.95
Moderately round bilge with flat after sections	2.10	2.33	2.45	2.60	3.0	3.40

The displacement figure required for these calculations is the actual weight of water which the boat displaces in normal service condition, reckoned in (Imperial) tons of 2240 lbs. Where the displacement is not known it may be found approximately by the following:

$$\text{Displacement (tons)} = \frac{L \times B \times D \times Cb}{W}$$

L = waterline length in feet
B = waterline beam in feet
D = draft in feet
Cb = block coefficient
W = 35 for seawater or 36 for fresh water (i.e. cu ft/ton)

The figure for the block coefficient is the only one that has to assessed, the others being obtainable by measurement of the vessel. The assessment is based on an approximation for the immersed volume of the hull. For given types of hull in lieu of actual calculation:

Type of hull		Block coefficient (Cb)
Planing	(A)	0.35–0.40
Semi-displacement	(B)	0.40–0.45
Displacement	(C)	0.45–0.55

Specimen midship and stern sections of different basic hull types are shown in Fig. 5.5. There can be many variations on these but the sections illustrated might help you to relate your own hull approximately so as to use the appropriate block coefficient figure for calculation.

In making the final assessment of the power requirement for a specific performance note should be taken of transmission losses. With a direct drive conventional gearbox and sterngear the losses will be small and confined to the propeller shaft bearings and gland; this should not amount to much more than 3%. But a reduction gearbox will add a further 3% and a V-drive gearbox can absorb 5%.

When using oil-hydraulic or water jet propulsion systems or a

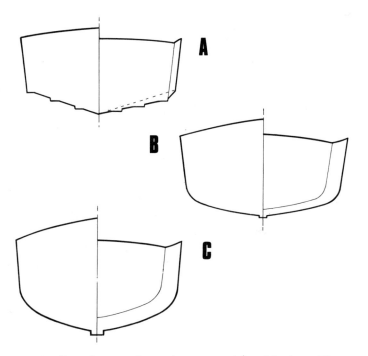

5.5   Hull sections to determine approximate block coefficient

sterndrive it should be noted that the losses are greater with these, and while various claims are made, which tend to be without the benefit of precise comparison, it is suggested that for a working approach to the assessment an efficiency loss of 5–10% above that of simple conventional sterngear be allowed. That is not to say that for many applications these losses will not be acceptable – in practice such transmissions may provide an overall advantage according to the kind of service envisaged.

6. Transmission

Marine gearboxes for pleasure craft are mostly of the type which is attached directly to the engine and becomes an integral part of the unit, but installations for large motor yachts may have a separate gearbox on its own mounting with a drive shaft from the power unit. V-drive and U-drive gearboxes are similarly arranged. The function of the gearbox or astern gear is to change the direction of rotation of the propeller shaft and also give an intermediate disengaged position. The gear train involved to accomplish this may be conventional with a secondary shaft to provide reverse rotation or it may be epicyclic, but in any case the gears always remain in mesh and they transmit or are freed from the drive by clutches; it is these which are engaged or otherwise when the gear lever is moved.

The operation of the clutch may be mechanical, in which case an external lever is provided, or it can be hydraulic. A gearbox operated by the latter means will have its own built-in oil pump and also generally its own oil cooler and filtration. Most of the small power units have mechanically operated gearboxes and the larger, multi-cylinder engines are usually hydraulically controlled. Besides ease of operation the hydraulic system gives the facility for remote control and also single-lever operation, if required, of both engine throttle and gearbox.

When reduction gearing is required it can either be incorporated in the main gear train (Fig. 6.1) or provided by separate gearing on the output shaft (Fig. 6.2), depending on the type of gearbox chosen. Opposite rotation of the propeller shafts for twin engine installations may be achieved via the reduction gearing, e.g. using gear drive in one reduction box and chain in the other. Some modern hydraulic boxes are designed to operate continuously on full power in either direction or can be supplied for either hand output. The example (Fig. 6.3) gives a 10° output shaft down angle which may be valuable for many installations.

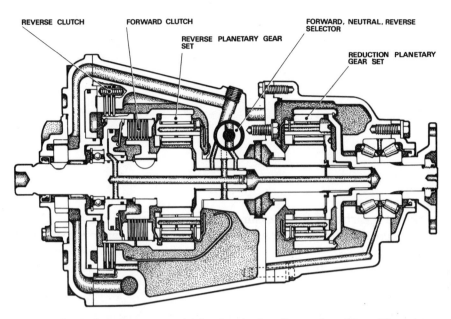

6.1   In-line, planetary reverse/reduction hydraulic gearbox (*Borg-Warner*)

6.2   Hy-Drive hydraulic gearbox with dropped reduction gear. Wortham
Blake. (*Author*)

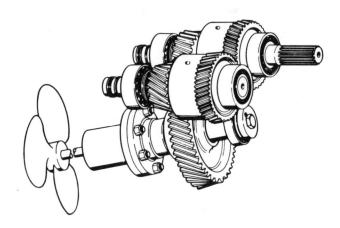

6.3   Twin Disc Model MG-502 hydraulic gearbox with 10° down angle on output shaft

V-drives are becoming increasingly popular for fast power cruisers; they offer space saving as well as putting the engines where they are least intrusive from the point of view of noise (Fig. 6.4). The V-drive gears may be housed at the output end of the gearbox or they can have a separate gearcase driven by a shaft from the gearbox. An alternative which gives almost the same configuration is the U-drive; in this the input and output shafts are parallel and it is therefore necessary to incorporate two universal joints in the shaft from the engine to the U-drive gearbox (Fig. 6.5). In the example shown a standard marine gearbox with ahead, astern and optional reduction ratios is adapted to U-drive by bringing both shafts out on the same side of the unit.

Besides having integral oil pumps to provide the power for gear control, the hydraulic box will, as mentioned, also have its own oil cooling arrangements via a heat exchanger using either raw water or an extension of the engine's freshwater cooling system as the exchange element. On the larger units oil pressure and temperature gauges enable a check to be kept on the oil circulation in the hydraulic gearbox in the same way as engine conditions are monitored. In the event of hydraulic failure an emergency 'lock-up' arrangement, whereby the ahead gear may be kept in engagement to get the vessel home, is usually available either as standard or an optional extra.

Gearboxes attached directly to the engine frequently have a torsionally resilient drive plate to cushion the drive from the power unit to

6.4 V drive on Mercury 225 petrol engine

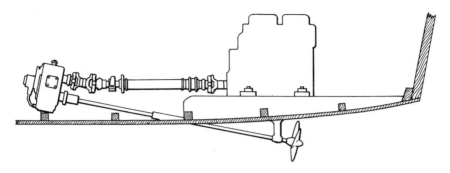

6.5   U-drive installation suitable for MG-509 U Twin Disc gearbox

the gearbox, and others which are mounted separately may have a flexible coupling on the gearbox input shaft.

The bearings on the ouput shaft of a marine gearbox are designed to take the thrust from the propeller; if therefore a flexible coupling is incorporated in the propeller shaft line it must either be of a type which will transmit thrust through to the gearbox or a separate thrust bearing must be fitted.

Engine installations in sailing yachts or motorsailers where the propeller is liable to be trailed for long periods might need to have a brake on the shaft to prevent rotation and incidentally to clamp the shaft in the position for least drag. The manufacturer's operating requirements for the gearbox should be checked – some are designed to tolerate continuous rotation, some have a built-in brake, some are approved for rotation but only for limited periods, and the manufacturer might recommend that the engine be run to circulate the oil after a stated number of hours trailing with rotation.

The line taken between the engine/gearbox and the stern tube bearing may be varied by the inclusion of one or more flexible couplings, by offset or dropped output shaft from the gearbox, or both. The question of whether one or two flexible couplings are required to properly meet differences between output and propeller shaft angles – and also the differences arising from flexible engine mountings in conjunction with a rigid stern tube bearing – is liable to provoke many answers. An approximate guide to satisfactory installation is that where the intention proposes a difference in alignment the difficulty in obtaining exact intersection of the shaft lines makes the fitting of two flexible couplings advisable. If metal universal joints are employed a pair *must* be fitted.

Where the consideration is to take up the movement of the engine on flexible mountings the deciding factor is the length of shaft between the gearbox and the stern tube bearing. One flexible coupling seems to be generally acceptable in conjunction with a rigid or solid stern tube bearing if the intervening shaft is 2ft or more in length, but if the shaft needs to be shorter than this to meet installation requirements another flexible coupling should be fitted. Failure to observe this may lead to a short life for the gearbox tailshaft bearing and oil seal or the propeller shaft in its stern bearings or the outer sterntube bearing even although this may be of the cutless type.

These considerations apply where a rigid inboard stern tube bearing is fitted; if the bearing and gland is of the floating type with a cutless rubber outer bearing it is possible to dispense with flexible couplings and have one solid flange coupling between the gearbox and the propeller shaft. Shaft logs with a floating gland for the propeller shaft do not have a supporting inboard bearing and thus the drive may be solid from the engine to the propeller with the flexibility of the gland accommodating differences in alignment brought about by movement of the engine on anti-vibration mountings.

If an engine is to be fitted with a solid coupling and a rigid stern tube bearing then it must also be solidly mounted, and accuracy in alignment is essential to the extent that with a wooden boat it is necessary to make the final adjustments when the vessel is in the water and has taken up its waterborne shape.

Whatever the nature of the transmission and sterngear it is essential that it should be aligned accurately, and the fitment of floating glands, flexible couplings, etc does not obviate the need for correct alignment with the engine at rest, otherwise excessive loads may be put on the whole of the transmission, and also the possibility of vibration will be greatly increased.

For sailing auxiliaries a controllable (c.p.) or variable pitch (v.p.) propeller can provide a suitable alternative to the conventional gearbox. The forward – neutral – reverse capability is given by propeller blades which can be rotated in the hub so as to alter the pitch from the forward to the reverse angle through an intermediate position where the blades are at right angles to the propeller shaft and therefore obtaining no 'bite' on the water. With some propellers of this type the forward pitch angle can be exceeded until the blades are in line with the propeller shaft, so reducing drag when the vessel is under sail. It will be noted that if the pitch is variable over a wide range the effect will be the same as that of a multi-ratio gearbox in that the load on the engine may be adjusted to suit various conditions. This can be of advantage when motor-sailing since the propeller pitch can be adjusted to give the best effect when some of the drive is being obtained from the sails.

The pitch of a c.p. propeller may be altered mechanically or hydraulically via a limited longitudinal movement of the propeller shaft or a sleeve on the shaft. Either pegs or pinions on the roots of the blades engage with an angular slot or a toothed rack, the longitudinal movement of which is translated into rotary movement on the blades. The mechanism is generally simple and robust, but due to the necessary incorporation of movement in the propeller hub restriction of the speed of rotation is more critical than with a solid propeller.

Because of the wide variation in engine loading which can be obtained with a c.p. propeller it is necessary to exercise some caution in use to ensure that the engine is not overloaded with an excessively coarse pitch setting or allowed to over-speed through the pitch being set too fine.

Another kind of propeller, but one which gives no adjustment for pitch or going astern, is the folding type where the blades are hinged so as to fold together and so minimize drag when it is being trailed. Rotation of the propeller shaft causes the blades to unfold through centrifugal force and they then have an angle of attack on the water and thrust is obtained. The attitude the blades take up when going astern may not lend itself to very efficient propulsion since the blades will be trying to pull themselves into the folded position. Propellers of this type are principally of interest for performance sailing craft where auxiliary propulsion efficiency may be sacrificed in the interest of minimum drag when under sail.

Propeller manufacturers are able to give an indication of suitable diameter and pitch for most installations, but in spite of this, where an installation is completely new in that there has been no experience with a similar boat and engine combination, it is often found possible to improve performance by experiment on either side of the data recommendation. The type of propeller employed – as distinct from the size – will vary considerably with the kind of vessel and engine installation (Fig. 6.6) but for the majority of motor cruisers and other power craft they are of the equipoise and turbine types, and the three-bladed configuration gives the best means of obtaining suitable pitch and diameter ratios for most.

Two-bladed propellers are frequently fitted to auxiliary installations in sailing craft and these are sometimes of the long-bladed, sailing,

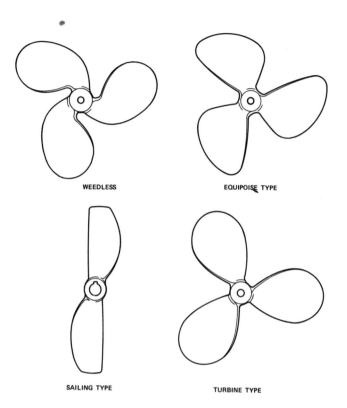

WEEDLESS

EQUIPOISE TYPE

SAILING TYPE

TURBINE TYPE

6.6   A selection of propeller types (*Gaines*)

or Swedish type which are designed to position themselves behind the deadwood when under sail. If the deadwood is thick enough to more or less obscure the blades the arrangement can cause vibration when the engine is running through interruption of the water flow to both blades simultaneously at every half revolution of the shaft.

In selecting a propeller the particulars required include: the type of boat, its dimensions, displacement, the shape of the stern and any restricting factors, e.g. the thickness of the deadwood in front of the propeller and the swing (diameter) which can be accommodated; the maximum and continuous rated bhp of engine and the corresponding rpm; and the reduction ratio, if any. Also the required direction of rotation of the propeller viewed from aft (handing) stated as clockwise or anticlockwise, taking into account change in direction of rotation which may be effected by a reduction gear, if fitted. With this

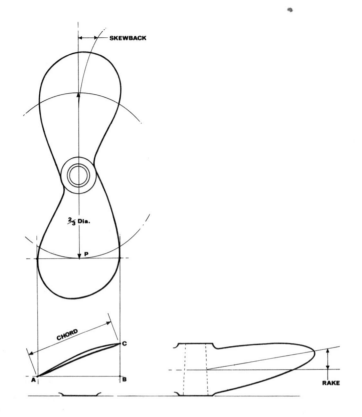

6.7 Finding the pitch of a propeller. AC is the width of the blade, CB a vertical line from the leading edge, and AB the width projected to a horizontal line. In turning the distance AB the advance neglecting slip is equal to CB. The circumference of a circle through P is equal to the diameter at P $\times \frac{22}{7}$ and as the pitch is the advance during one revolution, the pitch will bear the proportion to BC that the circumference has to AB, or:

$$\text{Pitch} = \frac{\text{BC} \times \text{circumference}}{\text{AB}}$$

information the propeller manufacturer is able to provide a recommendation as to size and type.

The practice when measuring the pitch of propeller blades is to refer to the angle at two-thirds diameter. To obtain the measurement the propeller is laid on a flat surface with the boss vertical (Fig. 6.7). The pitch at P which is on a circle scribed at two-thirds D may then be found as shown. The measurement is made at two-thirds the diameter because this is a mean of the pitch angle, which decreases from the root of the blade to the tip to account for the fact that the speed of the blade increases with diameter; thus the pitch angle is varied so that the whole length of the blade will make the same rate of advance through the water.

The calculation of the advance of the blade through the water in one revolution, which can be made from the pitch measurement, is a theoretical maximum which is not attainable in practice, and the difference between the theoretical and the actual advance is known as slip. The percentage of slip will vary considerable between different types of installation, and even supposing the optimum is achieved in the selection of a suitable propeller the slip to be expected will be not less than 10–15% for a light, planing hull, and it can be as much as 50% for a heavy displacement boat or an auxiliary installation. Propellers on displacement boats have lower efficiencies partly because they are operating in disturbed water in the wake of the vessel; lighter craft and planing boats move less water and the conditions are thus closer to the medium proposed by theory, but considerable losses still have to be accepted.

Most of the larger, multi-cylinder engines are given two ratings – continuous and intermittent. The intermittent rating will be the maximum bhp which the engine will deliver as stated by the manufacturer. The continuous rating will be somewhat less than this, and as implied the engine may be operated continuously at the power and rev/min given in the maker's data. Since a propeller can be selected to give the maximum efficiency at a certain rev/min it is necessary to decide whether the optimum efficiency shall be attained at continuous or intermittent rev/min. The type of boat largely indicates the decision. If it is a cruiser of a displacement type more likely to be cruised for long periods at steady but not maximum power, then a propeller chosen to match the continuous rating will be favoured. But if it is a semi-displacement or planing boat from which maximum performance for short periods may more often be demanded, a propeller to suit the intermittent rating may be chosen. Some engine manufacturers show propeller law curves on their engine performance graphs. These indicate the power absorption of propellers selected for different ratings with propeller matching at the recommended power and rev/min. (Fig. 6.8).

A suitable diameter for the propeller shaft can be ascertained by reference to the graph (Fig. 6.9). However, the graph does not accommodate extreme pitch angles and allowance must be made for the

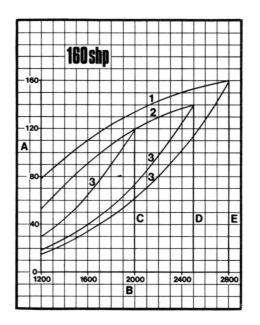

6.8 Engine performance graph with propeller law curves (*Perkins*)
Key

A	Power	shp	1 Mean intermittent output from gearbox output flange
B	Engine speed	rpm	
C	Max. continuous heavy duty rated speed	2000 rpm	2 Mean continuous output from gearbox output flange
D	Max. continuous medium duty rated speed	2500 rpm	3 Typical propeller law curves
E	Max. intermittent rated speed	2800 rpm	

heavier loading given by a high pitch/diameter ratio; similarly, some tolerance is possible for a propeller with the same diameter but having a fine pitch. It is recommended that the propeller shaft for a diesel engine installation be of slightly greater diameter than that for a petrol engine, given the same power and speed of rotation.

Shaft whip of any significance is not to be expected with any reasonably engineered installation having suitably stiff A or P brackets if the shaft is exposed, but whether the propeller is below the hull or in the deadwood the best operating conditions call for a tip clearance of not

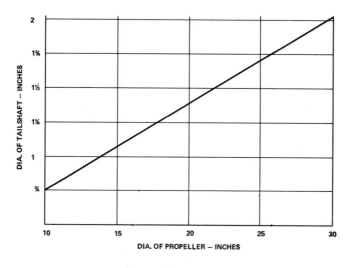

6.9   Shaft sizes for propeller diameters

less than 15% of the propeller diameter.

Where an engine is installed sufficiently far forward in the hull to call for a long shaft between gearbox and stern tube the need for an intermediate steady bearing must be considered. It is suggested that for shafts under 1 in diameter the unsupported length should not exceed 2ft 6in. Over this diameter the distance may be proportionately increased.

7. Sterndrives and Other Outdrives

This form of transmission may be variously called Z-drive, outdrive, inboard/outboard, outboard drive, or sterndrive; some manufacturers have their own names for the system, e.g. Aquamatic, Mercruiser, Transa-Drive, etc. For the purpose of this chapter we will call it sterndrive.

Sterndrive is available for a power range of from approximately 25 to 250 bhp and it is suitable for both petrol and diesel units, although the power rating of a given drive unit will be lower for diesel engines, which give higher transmission loadings than petrol units. The main advantages of the sterndrive are a readily obtained match of power unit and transmission and simplified installation involving only one hole in the transom of the boat through which all mechanism and controls operate. It can be fitted to nearly any boat which has a suitable stiffened transom but is more often seen in planing and semi-displacement craft, particularly in combination with a high power petrol unit, and for runabouts, fast dayboats and light displacement cruisers where the high power/weight ratio is of advantage. However, larger craft including displacement vessels and workboats may use a sterndrive with diesel power and gain a considerable amount of space as well as economy thereby. In space saving and lower noise levels the sterndrive shares some of the attributes of the V-drive in putting the power unit right aft where it is less intrusive.

Trim and tilt arrangements for the outboard are much the same as on the larger outboard engines, and in common with these the efficiency is somewhat lower than that of a conventional sterngear, since excluding such losses as may be incurred through putting the power through a Z turn, there is the larger matter of drag on the immersed part of the unit. Various efficiencies in comparison with ordinary sterngear have been quoted and the figure suggested by the builder of one popular range of power boats is a loss of up to 10%, but precise information is lacking.

It is usual for the whole of the outboard part of the sterndrive to be steerable, but there are exceptions. The Volvo Penta Aquamatic 750 has only the lower part of the unit steerable, and another example, the Ocean 60, is not steerable at all as far as the drive is concerned but has a rudder attached.

The general arrangement of one of the larger sterndrive units is shown in the cutaway drawing of the Aquamatic 280 (Fig. 7.1). It will be seen that the lower end of the drive is very similar to that of the bigger outboard engines with the cooling water intake at the bottom of the leg and a large cavitation plate. In this case the exhaust is taken through the plate which is a hollow casting, but in other examples, as the Mercruiser, the exhaust is taken through the propeller hub and follows the design of the Mercury outboard engines. Another difference between these two drives is the location of the gears and clutch for forward, neutral and reverse; in the Aquamatic they are in the top of the drive casing whereas in the Mercruiser they are in the lower unit (Fig. 7.2). For twin installations the direction of propeller rotation can be changed on the Aquamatic by relocating the clutch link rod. There is a hydraulically operated lift and trim device built into the mounting collar. In conjunction with the AQ 225 Volvo Penta engine this sterndrive will transmit up to 225 bhp at 4400 rpm. Three gear ratios are available via selection of the bottom bevel and pinion.

The smallest and most popular Aquamatic, the Model 100, is suitable for small displacement boats as well as planing craft, e.g. it can be coupled to the Volvo MD2B diesel engine which delivers 25 bhp at 2500 rpm, and the same unit used with the Volvo petrol AQ 115 will cope with 115 bhp at 5100 rpm.

Mercruiser sterndrives are made in a large number of models from 120 up to 225 bhp. Power trim is standard on all of them and the two largest units of 225 and 255 bhp have electrically controlled hydraulic transmission coupled to eight-cylinder V8 power units. This configuration gives a very compact installation for the high power available. The smaller engines in the range have four and six cylinders in line. The larger Mercruisers have high power/weight ratios of better than 5 lbs per hp.

OMC also have a wide range of sterndrive/power units from 90 up to 255 bhp of four and six cylinders in line and V8 configuration, offering all of the power control features which enable optimum performance to be obtained from the drive, and it may be noted here that the requirements for trim control apply equally to outboard engines and sterndrives. Use of the trim control will get a planing boat over the hump and onto the plane more quickly and it also enables

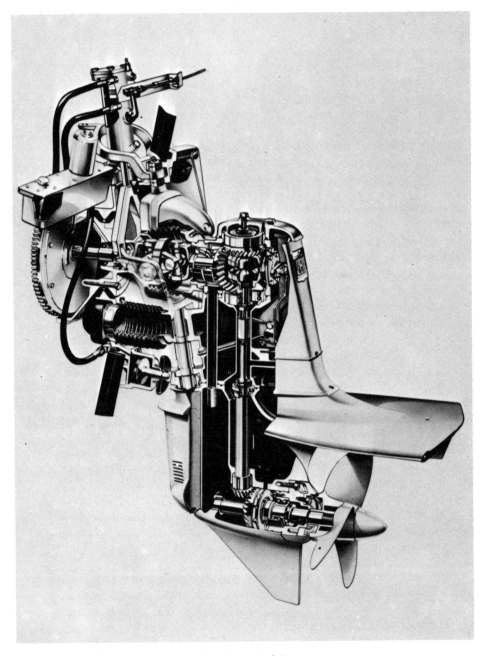

7.1   Volvo Penta Aquamatic 280 sterndrive

7.2   Mercruiser 888 sterndrive

adjustment to be made for sea conditions and load. With the bow trimmed down the boat will accelerate more rapidly onto the plane and for maximum speed the bow may be lifted to give the minimum hull resistance.

Enfield Z-drive transom units are made in a range up to over 220 bhp and they are suitable for Ford, Perkins, Renault, Volkswagen, JGM Seadrive, Mercedes and Yanmar engines. The JGM Seadrive petrol unit of 30 bhp which incorporates the Enfield 130 Z-drive makes a compact power/transmission combination for smaller vessels (Fig. 7.3). The Enfield Model 130 weighs only 90 lbs but will transmit up to 78 bhp diesel and 130 bhp petrol. It can be supplied with either manual or hydraulic trim/tilt facility.

Transa-Drive sterndrives, which are claimed to have a very efficient underwater shape for minimum drag, are made in models suitable for 20 to 220 bhp petrol and 10 to 140 bhp diesel. These also can be supplied with manual or hydraulic trim and lift. The latter system incorporates a hydraulic lock valve which permits the lower unit to be very sensitive to underwater obstructions when in neutral or for-

7.3   JGM Seadrive with BLMC 1100P petrol engine and Enfield 130 Z-drive

ward gear; accidental contact causes the leg to lift immediately without having to overcome resistance from a pressure relief valve, necessarily set at high pressure in many units so that the boat may go astern without the leg lifting.

The BMW marine petrol engine is available with an Aquamatic unit in two models of 115 and 180 bhp. This is of course a marinized road vehicle engine as is also the Dolphin Vegamatic, but the Vegamatic has the Ford 2401 diesel coupled to an Enfield 130 Z-drive; it offers 64.5 bhp maximum with diesel economy and an inclusive weight of only 649 lbs.

Manoeuvrability with a steerable sterndrive is very good under power, as may be expected from being able to turn the propeller thrust in the required direction, but there is very little steering capability when the engine is out of gear. With twin drives it is necessary to be able to tilt the leg of an engine which goes out of operation since otherwise the drag may have a crippling effect on the remaining unit. The effect will of course vary from boat to boat according to power, weight and hull shape; the remaining engine can suffer from excessive propeller slip, or an inability to achieve sufficient rev/min, either of which may handicap a planing boat enough to reduce it to displacement speed.

Other examples of inboard/outboard drives are the 'thru the hull' units where the drive is taken through the bottom of the hull. The Volvo Penta Sailboat Drive is one of these which may be coupled to either a small petrol or diesel power unit and the GMS Marine Drive Unit is another, which also has the facility for shaft length adjustment to accommodate different hulls (Fig. 7.4). The GMS drive is suitable for up to 50 bhp petrol and 40 bhp diesel power. These drives offer some simplicity in installation, if the draft permits their use, since as with sterndrive there are no alignment problems, and no likelihood of leakage. The Volvo drive is supplied as an engine package with its own plastic bed which can be sawn to fit the bottom of the boat; the engines are either the MB10A 15 hp petrol or the MD6A 10 hp diesel (Fig. 7.5). Solid or folding propellers may be fitted.

7.4   GMS Marine adjustable 'through the hull' drive

7.5   Volvo Penta MB10A/100S Sailboat Drive

8. Water Jet Units

The origins of water jet or reaction propulsion are much earlier in boat history than may be popularly appreciated. H Philip Spratt in his interesting book *The Birth of the Steamboat* records that the principle of water reaction as a method of propulsion was first patented in Britain in 1661, but the first application of the principle (using steam power) was by the American, James Rumsey. From examination of the drawing reproduced in Mr Spratt's book it seems that we would find it difficult today to better the elegance and economy of James Rumsey's design which, apart from a couple of non-return valves, appears to have had only one moving part.

To describe it briefly, a cylinder was mounted vertically in the boat with its bottom end open to the water via a non-return valve. Another cylinder, of slightly larger diameter, stood on top of this and concentric with the other; thus the cylinder head of one was the base for the other and through this passed a piston rod with an integral piston at top and bottom. Steam from a primitive pot boiler passed into the base of the upper cylinder, forcing the top piston upwards; the bottom piston following suit, sucked in water through the bottom of the boat and into the lower cylinder. At the top of the upper piston stroke the steam was exhausted and the piston was forced down by atmospheric pressure. At this point the non-return valve in the bottom of the boat closed through pressure of water behind it and the water in the lower cylinder was forced through a duct, via another non-return valve, to the stern of the vessel where it was discharged below the waterline to give propulsive effort. There could hardly be anything more simple!

In 1787 there were trials on the Potomac and the boat made 4 mph against the current. In 1788 another prototype was built at Dover. This had a 24in diameter pump working at about 20 strokes per minute and a discharge duct or trunk 6in square. It was tried on the Thames and made 4 knots against wind and tide.

So it would seem that although the method of moving the water within the unit has changed, water jet reaction as a basic propulsion principle led the propeller by about a century.

No doubt a great many owners when giving thought to the manner in which their boat is to be driven tend to ignore anything other than variations of conventional transmission of which the general efficiency is known. The question of comparative efficiency is still rather foggy, and perhaps the enthusiasm of water jet proponents should lead them to obtain more obvious indications of efficiency vis-a-vis an ordinary propeller drive. How one goes about this is perhaps only clear by practical means, and the example given many years ago when the paddle steamer and the screw-driven vessel had their tug of war might serve again to convince more readily than several pages of graphs and thrust figures.

Provided that the water is not required to go round too many corners, there seems to be little reason why a jet unit should not give much the same efficiency as an exposed propeller, if correctly matched to the power available. A ducted fan is not normally less efficient than one with exposed blades, but it is probably wrong to try to take these analogies too far, as some makers of water jet units do, by instancing aircraft jets as similar examples in operation. There is little to compare between the two and the suggestion is misleading.

The basic principle of the modern water jet unit is that it draws in water through an orifice which is normally flush with the bottom of the hull, and an impeller accelerates the flow and discharges it through a tailpipe. The action of accelerating the water flow causes the usual reaction on the impeller blades and this thrust is transmitted via the impeller shaft to a thrust bearing at the forward end of the jet casing (Fig. 8.1). Several advantages will be apparent: the jet unit is complete, and apart from making the necessary holes in the bottom of the boat and the transom it does not need lining up in any way; transmission of thrust is incorporated in the unit; in most cases, supposing engine and jet unit have suitable characteristics there need be no gearing between the power unit and the jet. The jet may also be used for steering and reverse, and most units are designed to accommodate this. A feature which is attractive in crowded water sport areas is that the impeller is completely enclosed and cannot imperil anyone in the water; it is also suited to shallow water.

The usual means of going astern dispenses with a gearbox. A movable bucket or cowl is arranged to redirect the flow of water from the

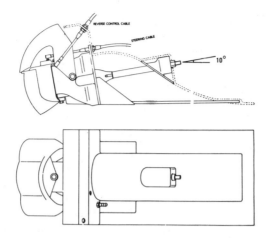

8.1   HP6 water jet unit for displacement boats up to 25 hp input and planing boats to 45 hp *(UA Engineering Ltd)*

tailpipe so that it is discharged forward, and the effect of this water pressure against the body of water in which the boat is moving causes an excellent braking effect which, if prolonged, will move the boat astern (Fig. 8.2). It will be apparent that the efficiency going astern is very much reduced because to an extent the unit is being made to work against itself.

Steering is a somewhat simpler matter; deflector plates are employed to direct the water from the tailpipe to one side or the other and the jet impinging against the plates plus any direct reaction against the water in which the boat is moving causes the stern of the vessel to be moved in the required direction (Fig. 8.3). The higher the speed the more sensitive and positive is the movement, but since the jet creates no torsional bias or 'throw' of the stern to either side it is possible to over-come any low speed wander by brief acceleration of the engine and appropriate movement of the steering. The usual method of removing swirl from the water as it emerges from the impeller is to incorporate vanes in the tailpipe which straighten out the flow.

There are a considerable number of variations in detail between different makes of water jet, but the two basic types are: low volume, high pressure, high rev/min units, and high volume, low pressure, low rev/min installations. In general terms the former are suitable for light, high speed boats fitted with petrol engines (which may be car engine conversions), and the latter are for bigger, heavier craft and suitable

8.2   Berkeley jet showing reverse deflector over tailpipe (*Eric Coltham*)

for use with diesel engines. High rev/min jets can be quite modest in cost in the smaller sizes; as an example, a complete unit which will take up to 45 bhp may cost less than £100, but bigger jets and low speed units for diesels of 150 bhp or over may well cost more than a conventional gearbox and sterngear.

Beyond the basic type difference there are single and multi-stage units, the latter generally being built up with two or more standard impeller and casing sections connected in tandem. Impeller design can vary greatly from a reasonably straightforward wide-bladed propeller operating in a duct of constant diameter, to examples which are more akin to a multi-start helical screw turning in either a parallel or a tapered duct. This concerns axial flow types, but there are also what are known as mixed flow types where the water is accelerated by both axial and centrifugal movement; these units have rather more complex impellers working in tapered bowl casings. Dowty, UA and Hamilton offer examples of the propeller type, Castoldi use the helical screw in a slightly tapered housing (Fig. 8.4), and Jacuzzi and Berkeley are mixed flow units.

8.3   Twin Dowty jets. Note steering deflector plates on near jet and reverse flow cowl partly down on the other. (*Eric Coltham*)

In all of them the duct below the boat is arranged to sweep up gently to the impeller housing and is of adequate size to meet the demand from the impeller at maximum rpm. Tailpipe diameters vary according to the characteristics and power of the unit and the final exit of the water may be either between deflector plates for steering, as described, or it may be through a pipe which can be swivelled to achieve a similar effect. In the latter case the section of the pipe is such that restriction is not offered to the exit flow through lateral movement across the mouth of the tailpipe nozzle.

Outboard engines may also be fitted to produce a water jet instead of using a conventional propeller. They gain, as with an inboard jet unit, from being safer in use, but otherwise there seems to be less to promote them in preference to an ordinary outboard engine except that they need very little immersion and need not project much below the bottom of the boat. There are examples of both axial flow and centrifugal units; the Warren Jet and the Deflectajet are axial flow but

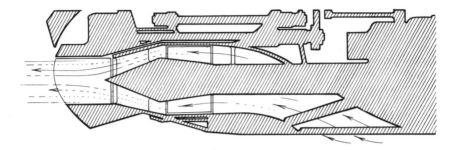

8.4   Section through Castoldi jet

in both units the water is drawn up and deflected through a right angle after being accelerated by the impeller.

Examples of standard jet-driven cruisers are few in the UK as yet (the Hunter Jet cruiser is a current example) but with the general increase of interest in the system it may not be long before it is offered as an option in larger craft – jets are employed outside the UK in a number of work boats and barges – as well as having current use in runabouts and dayboats. Messrs Tyler had *Jet Slipper* at a recent London International Boat Show. This is a Nelson 34ft fibreglass displacement-type hull powered by two Ford Thornycroft 140 bhp diesels driving a pair of two-stage Dowty 12in water jets. She is capable of 20 knots and opinion is that the overall efficiency is within 2% of that of a conventional drive.

The availability of secondhand car engines at low cost must make the water jet very attractive to DIY powerboat builders since the smaller jets are well suited to the higher rev/min at which it is usual for car engines to develop their power. Thus full efficiency may be obtained without reduction gearing, and this, combined with a built-in thrust bearing and simplified installation, should have an increasingly wide appeal.

The list below shows some of the range of water jet units now available.

OUTBOARDS
   Deflectajet   1 bhp
   Warren Jet   2.6 and 4.1 bhp

INBOARDS

Warren Jet	1.9 and 2.5 bhp
Shipelle Saifjet	3–20 bhp
Parker	26 bhp
UA 6	25–45 bhp
Hotchkiss	4–400 bhp
Berkeley	7–330 bhp
Hamilton	50–400 bhp
Dowty	100–500 bhp
Jacuzzi	80–1000 bhp
Castoldi	10–500 bhp

9. Hydraulic Drives

Fluid drives for marine use have not had much of an appeal to date; such examples as have appeared in the past have often proved workable, but failure to convince has caused them to fade gently from the market. In the marine sector the principal advantage offered, which is that of complete freedom of location for the power unit, has not outweighed the inability to pump oil with anywhere near the same efficiency as is given by a conventional transmission.

There are occasions when some reduction in performance may be accepted because the design of the major unit does not permit any other method, and if the job is sufficiently important it is possible that development will be applied with small regard to expense so as to raise the efficiency of the principle to an acceptable level. This is what appears to have happened in the case of the hydraulic drives now made by Volvo Flygmotor; the unit now being produced was developed in America for use in rocketry and space projects and it is formidably potent for its size. It has already been proved under the most stringent conditions, and Volvo confidently assert that 10,000 hours may be obtained from a unit before any attention is needed – which is longer than most marine engines in yachts will run in their lifetimes.

The first requirement is an efficient pump and the next an efficient hydraulic motor; one of the virtues of the Volvo unit is that it may be either pump or motor, as the same unit serves with similar efficiency in both capacities. The basic pump/motor consists of a casing enclosing a cylinder drum, pistons and a swash plate mounted on heavy duty bearings; the drum contains five small cylinders with pistons connected by ball joints to the swash plate, and the axis of the plate lies at an angle of 40° to the axis of the cylinder drum (Fig. 9.1). The pistons are driven by oil entering the cylinders successively via kidney-shaped ports in the base of the drum; the cylinder drum and the swash plate have a meshing bevel gear so that rotation of the swash plate caused by the successive

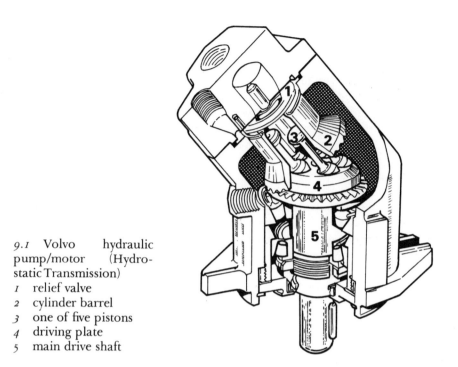

9.1 Volvo hydraulic pump/motor (Hydro-static Transmission)
1   relief valve
2   cylinder barrel
3   one of five pistons
4   driving plate
5   main drive shaft

pressure of the five pistons also causes rotation of the cylinder drum; by this means the kidney port in each cylinder head is brought round in turn over the pressure port in the motor housing, which is connected directly to the pressure line from the pump.

There are actually two ports sited 180° apart in the motor housing below the cylinder drum, one for pressure and the other for scavenging, but it will be seen that since the arrangement is symmetrical a reversal of the flow through these ports will cause the motor to run in the reverse direction but with equal efficiency.

We have of course been describing the operation of the unit as a motor: the description remains the same for the pump but in this case the swash plate journal (which in the motor is the output shaft) becomes a driven member coupled directly to the output shaft of an engine. The power of the engine is transmitted via the pump and high pressure oil lines to the motor – which within limits may be put as close to or as far away from from the power unit as is convenient. The loss incurred by longer pressure hose is about 1% per metre run; the overall loss for the pump/motor system about 13% which compares with around

3–10% for a conventional gearbox transmission, dependent upon whether direct drive, reduction, or V-drive.

These hydraulic units are made in five sizes to cope with the transmission of from 13 up to 86 hp. Size C-19 which is the middle unit in the range and measures only approximately $6\frac{1}{2} \times 5 \times 4\frac{1}{2}$ in – it can easily be held in the hand – will manage inputs of up to 34 hp as a pump, and a similar unit at the other end working as a motor will deliver a torque of 52.8 lbs ft. A measure of the power being handled by such small units is indicated by the size of the bearings required on the input end of the pump or the output end of the motor – whichever way you care to look at it; about one half of the casing, size as above, is taken up by two very big taper roller bearings and the shaft for this size is 1in in diameter. An input oil pressure to the motor of 3500 lb/sq in or more removes the necessity for any kind of mechanical thrust bearing beneath the cylinder drum, the bottom face of which floats in an annulus which is open to the full line pressure.

Because the pistons driving the swash plate are integral with their connecting rods they have to be permitted some angular movement in two planes besides their reciprocating function – hence the necessity for a ball joint connection to the swash plate; to achieve this angular freedom the pistons instead of being cylindrical are truncated spheres with a single piston ring slot on or about the maximum diameter into which a convex ground piston ring is fitted. By this means the piston and ring assembly is fulfilling its proper function in sealing the cylinder although reciprocating with the connecting rod at a continuously varying angle. Pressure of the piston ring against the cylinder wall is balanced to some extent by the size of the slot, which permits oil to get behind the ring, and the angle which the face of the convex ground ring makes with the cylinder wall; the pressure from two directions gives a floating effect which minimizes ring and cylinder wear. A further refinement in manufacture is that the cylinder walls are roll surfaced prior to gas hardening.

The ball joints with the swash plates are also carefully considered in that they are ground and lapped until a 100% bearing area is achieved; this standard of accuracy combined with operation in a high pressure oil bath ensures a service life which is way beyond that of most mechanical assemblies. An attempted destruction test by continuous reversal of the unit under load for 8000 hours resulted only in the failure of three lever control units of otherwise good reputation.

Either a special hydraulic oil or a conventional, light mineral lubricating oil can be used with these pump/motor units, the oil reservoir with injector to boost supply to the pump being bolted onto the engine in lieu of a conventional gearbox (Fig. 9.2).

One of the features of this installation is that the power unit may not only be located out of the way, but it can also be mounted so flexibly that the minimum of vibration is transmitted to the hull; cushioning of this order is barely feasible with mechanical drives. Another feature is that although response to the throttle and reversal is prompt, the system seems to afford some cushioning to the take-up of the drive. With a separate throttle central lever permitting the engine speed to be set without reference to the ahead/astern control the latter is only switching oil, and with the engine set for a fast tickover a nice control is obtained for close manoeuvres using only the ahead/astern valve lever.

A relief valve protects the system against overload, e.g. if the propeller is fouled it will cut in until the load is reduced to the rated figure.

The assembly of motor, shaft, sterntube and propeller obviously needs no lining up and the installation angle can be literally anything that is required. This sort of versatility could open up new possibilities

9.2   Thornycroft type 154 diesel with ARS Volvo hydraulic drive. (*Author*)

for owners finding difficulty in applying power to particular kinds of craft, and two examples spring to mind: the sailing cruiser/racer with not much room in its afterbody for either installation or subsequent maintenance of an auxiliary with conventional sterngear; second, a suggestion which could apply very well to motorsailer catamarans, is to have a drive unit in each hull powered by a single engine located amidships or anywhere else convenient. It is a feature of this method of powering that the drive may be divided up between several driven units, that is to say, one or more propellers, plus halyard or sheet winches, anchor windlass etc. The effect of division with more than one driven unit in operation simultaneously is to lower the rpm but not the torque which would be expected normally at that rpm; e.g. if one driven unit runs at 1000 rpm, two will run at 500 rpm, four at 250 rpm and so on.

British hydraulic drives are available for larger engines. The axial piston motors made by E W Marine are classically simple in design and operation, employing a fixed swash plate with a maximum of nine axially disposed pistons in a cylinder drum which is integral with the propeller shaft (it is possible to vary the design by having a lesser number of pistons for lower power requirements). Thus the whole of the mechanism is in line and it is possible to reduce the bearing loads imparted by the propeller by having shaft bearings at both ends of the piston/cylinder assembly; there is a long plain bearing forward and a plain bearing and a heavy duty ball bearing behind which takes both radial loading and the propeller thrust. Provision is made for two basic installations, one with the motor outboard in a streamlined 'thru the hull' casing (Fig. 9.3), and the other as an inboard unit with conventional sterngear. The outboard unit is naturally cooled by the surrounding water, but it is necessary on the inboard installation to employ water jacketing around the motor, fed via a bleed-off from the engine freshwater cooling system.

The motor is driven by an axial piston variable displacement pump working at up to 4000 lb/sq in which is charged by another smaller pump at 100 lb/sq in. Variable delivery is effected by altering the angle of the swash plate in the pump so as to increase or decrease the piston stroke. Due to the use of a charge pump the oil reservoir can be quite small. The 'gearing' between the pump and the motor depends upon their respective capacities, thus if the capacity of the motor is fixed and that of the pump is variable (and reversable) an infinitely variable ratio is given either ahead or astern. It is possible to use the pump control regardless of engine speed and this enables

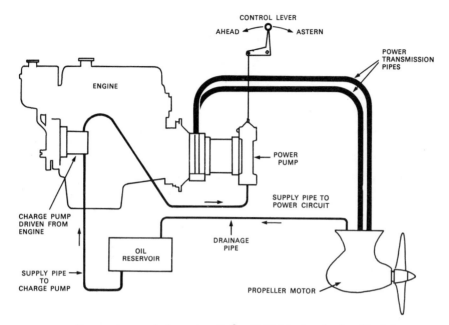

9.3   Power transmission circuit for E W Marine hydraulic drive.

propeller speed to be adjusted in order to absorb the engine power available at any rpm. This is one of the advantages of the hydrostatic drive, which tends to cancel out differences of efficiency based on the optimum performance of a conventional engine/gearbox fixed ratio installation.

It will be apparent that it is also possible to obtain complete variation in boat speed and direction (ahead – astern) when coupled to an engine set to run at a governed speed; experiment with the control level in these circumstances is fascinating since there is no loading on the lever in any position and variation of speed and direction of the propeller is light and precise.

The ability of these motors to operate efficiently at reduced rpm on lower volumes and with only proportional loss of torque enables one model to have a considerable range of application, e.g. Model 25 which will cater for a maximum of 70 bhp at 2000 rpm will also operate efficiently at 1000 rpm powered by an engine producing 40 bhp max. As with other hydraulic drives, the delivery from the pump may be split to two motors if required.

The engineering of both the pump and the motor unit is sufficiently robust to outlive most engines, for although the tolerances are small, complete immersion in oil ensures a longevity beyond the needs of any ordinary usage. The piston clearance is 0.0003in and there are no piston rings, but the length of the piston – approximately 3D – gives an effective oil seal, and there are four anti-lock grooves which equalize the pressure around the piston diameter. High pressure oil enters and evacuates the cylinders via ports in the bottom of the cylinder drum, and the base of the drum is supported from metallic contact against the stationary port face both by the line oil pressure and the propeller thrust bearing. A relief valve between the pressure lines prevents damage to the system in the event of a fouled propeller.

The pistons make liaison with the swash plate via ball joints in the piston heads which carry pads that are kept in continuous touch with the plate; the centres of the pads are recessed and a pressure oil drilling via the hollow piston enables them to float on the surface of the swash-plate without metal-to-metal contact. Springs below the pistons guard from damage through dry running by keeping the pads up against the plate. Swash plate angles of $14\frac{1}{2}°$ and $11\frac{1}{2}°$ are employed, the latter giving a shorter stroke for high speed units.

Pressure inside the casing of the unit is about 10 lb/sq in, adequate to give low pressure lubrication to the bearings and also to ensure that in the event of leakage it will be outwards and seawater will not enter. The joint faces of the casing are sealed with rubber O-rings and liquid jointing. A cup-type rubber seal is located on the propeller shaft behind the after bearing.

Another range of hydraulic transmissions is marketed by Enway Engineering catering for from 15 up to 164 bhp; these have similar pump and hydraulic motor systems to the British-made units described earlier, with a variable displacement swash plate pump and a fixed displacement motor. In a series named 15, 18 and 20/25 transmissions they have all the installation advantages common to the others. An efficiency curve for the 18 series indicates an overall efficiency of approximately 80% in the transmission of 25 to 49 bhp with the highest efficiency (about 83%) at the lower power.

10. Installation

Power units for larger vessels will be installed with the benefit of professional experience, but for those who take a hand in putting the machinery into a powerboat or auxiliary of more modest size the following notes may be useful.

Proper installation of the power unit is essential for reliable performance. In some cases, as with sterndrives, water jet units and hydraulic propulsion, the transmission either becomes a unit with the power source or the alignment of one need have no reference to the other, but with conventional transmission and sterngear correct alignment is vital. This applies whether flexible or rigid couplings are fitted in the shaft line, and it cannot be over-emphasized that flexible couplings and floating stern glands are not intended to accommodate permanent misalignment. Correct alignment of a transmission where there is flexibility in engine mounts, coupling or stern gland may be rather more difficult than lining up a rigid installation since error may not make itself so readily apparent, but unless two flexible couplings are fitted to accommodate a designed difference in output and propeller shaft angles accuracy in alignment is still important.

Generally speaking, engine bearers can rarely be too massive and they should always be of stout enough section to give complete rigidity to the installation; similarly, their attachment to the hull should be beyond reproach with adequate cross-chocking and a good weight of glass matting over, where wooden bearers are fitted into a fibreglass hull. The bearers should also be as long as conveniently possible so as to spread the load throughout the hull.

As engine alignment is important to smooth running and reliability, so is environment to performance. The ambient temperature of an engineroom or space becomes of some importance when the engine air intakes are within the engine compartment, as they often are on small craft. There are two considerations: the adequacy of the air supply and its temperature. It has been calculated that an internal combustion engine may use approximately $2\frac{1}{4}$ cu ft/min of air per bhp. A duct to supply this amount needs an internal area of about 1 sq in for every 2 bhp, e.g. an engine developing 50 bhp would require an air duct 5in square or the equivalent area. This would be for air entering the engine and at a temperature of not more than about 85°F. Because of the lower density of air with increasing temperature it can be reckoned that there will be a loss of 2% in engine efficiency for every 10° above the temperature at which the engine was rated.

When considering the elevated temperatures which are frequently encountered in enginerooms it becomes clear that an engine in such an environment is being effectively de-rated even supposing the flow of air to the intake is adequate: an engineroom temperature of over 100°F, which is not unusual, can take as much efficiency from the engine as the total friction losses accountable to a conventional gearbox and sterngear. It is therefore of some significance that the engine has air not only in sufficient volume for both aspiration and cooling as determined by the ducting, but also preferably at a temperature not much higher than that of the air outside the boat. Humidity also affects engine output but there is little that can be done about it.

It is advisable when choosing an engine to ascertain the basis of the power figure quoted. Two ratings sometimes quoted are SAE and DIN. The SAE rating is not a very useful indication because it refers to the output which the engine achieves when it is running stripped of all but its essential equipment. The DIN rating is more informative because it gives the bhp developed when the engine is fitted with its usual auxiliary equipment such as generator, etc. Some engine builders make the situation clear by referring to shp (shaft horsepower) and this is the most useful indication because it gives the power available at the output shaft with the engine in its standard installed condition, including a direct drive gearbox, if fitted.

Many engines built on the Continent are available elsewhere and it should be noted that the metric unit for horsepower, given as CV, PS or HK, is slightly lower than the British/American unit. One bhp is equivalent to 1.014 metric horsepower. (See Appendix.)

Ambient temperature in the engineroom should also be considered in relation to other equipment installed there. Electrical components, wiring and monitoring and control systems may all suffer deterioration or malfunction through prolonged high-temperature conditions. Adequate engineroom ventilation is desirable for a number of reasons and if a blower or fan is fitted some further consideration should be given to its operation. The temperature in an engine compartment normally rises when the engine is stopped since the coolant is no longer circulating and the residual heat is given off into the surrounding atmosphere. If the ventilating blower is wired so as to operate only when the engine is running there will be nothing to stop a rise in engineroom temperature when it is stopped, and temperatures as high as 180°F have been recorded in these conditions. It is therefore preferable to arrange the switching of the blower so that it can be run independently of the engine, and its use can then include a period before start up (to clear residual gases from batteries, evaporating fuel, etc), and the high temperature period after the engine has stopped. If only one fan is employed it is preferable to use it as an extractor, but of course an intake duct or ducts of adequate size must still be provided.

Incidentally, this waste engine heat which needs to be dispersed can be put to very good use in a cruiser with a freshwater cooled engine; a small additional heat exchanger will give free domestic hot water when the engine is running and for a long time after it has stopped.

The installation of a water cooled engine means one or more holes being cut in the hull; every hole which is below the waterline should have a seacock as well as a properly installed skin fitting. In most cases a seacock will be supplied complete with its skin fitting. Seacocks and piping have considerable weight and when this is set in motion by vibration an undesirable amount of flexing can occur in the hull skin around the fitting. Small fibreglass cruisers which have fairly light lay-ups may be particularly prone to the effect; consequently, each skin fitting should be mounted on a fitted, wide marine plywood pad which has been glassed over and bonded to the hull. The seacock should be bedded onto the pad with a non-hardening marine sealant. As a suggestion, a reasonable size of pad for a 1in bore seacock would be about 6in square.

Piping from tanks to engines should preferably be copper for petrol installations and fuel cocks should be fitted on the tanks. Non-combustible, metal flexible piping is obtainable for engines on flexible mountings and to reduce vibration in fuel lines. If, as to be preferred, the tanks and engines are in separate bays or compartments the integrity of the bulkhead in between can be maintained and the pipe system made more secure by using bulkhead unions to couple the fuel supply where it passes through instead of a continuous pipe passing through a hole in the bulkhead. If a continuous pipe is used it should be protected by a rubber grommet where it passes through the hole.

Fuel tanks for petrol may be copper, brass, steel, galvanized steel or stainless steel, but only steel, stainless steel or aluminium should be used for diesel fuel. Fibreglass tanks are acceptable only if made with self-quenching resin to BS 476. Tanks of more than 20 gallons capacity should incorporate baffles.

Engine exhaust arrangements should follow the manufacturer's recommendation; unusual systems which give rise to excessive back-pressure will also reduce the power output.

Diesel exhausts, after water cooling, can be conveniently installed with flexible rubber piping and mufflers, but dry exhausts or petrol engine exhausts will need to have a flexible metal bellows inserted in the pipe run from the engine when the unit is flexibly mounted. Copper and its alloys may be used for petrol engine exhaust systems but are not suitable for diesel exhausts; the materials for these are iron, steel, stainless steel or synthetic rubber (the latter after cooling by water injection).

Auxiliary engines in sailing vessels when situated below the water-line will need a large bend or swan neck in the exhaust pipe to obtain a fall to its exit overside. A drain cock should be fitted in the bottom bend. The system is probably more conveniently arranged by having instead a riser pipe on the engine with a water injection box on the top at sufficient height to give a straight fall of pipe to overside (Fig. 1.6).

Engine controls are tending increasingly towards the push-pull cable type such as Teleflex Morse. Very large motor yachts are now so equipped and the range available is suited to boats of all sizes from small launches up. These controls have several advantages: they can be taken in any direction, they have the minimum of lost movement, and they can be of almost any length without any increase in backlash. The only necessary condition in their fitting is that the bends in the cable shall not be too acute and that the proper angle of attack is made on the lever to be operated.

Electrical batteries should be secured in wood or plastic non-conductive trays. Large battery installations should have a canopy to trap fumes and a vent overside. Considered as a significant weight they should be installed centrally if possible and as low in the hull as is consistent with reasonable environment (keeping them clear of bilge water) and accessibility for service and removal. Starter cables should be kept as short as possible, and in the case of twin engine installations it is preferable to reserve one bank of batteries for starting both engines, using the other for powering the ship's supplies of lighting, etc. By this means the use of electrical equipment for domestic or navigational purposes can never drain all of the power for starting, but a paralleling switch should be incorporated for emergencies and an isolating master switch should be fitted in the main cable from each bank of batteries.

All electrical wiring in the engine space should be kept away from hot spots (engine exhaust, etc) and moving parts and also secured well up above the bilge.

Fire protection systems can be put into three categories: manual (hand extinguishers), automatic (self-monitoring) and remote controlled, which can be with or without monitoring. For an engine bay perhaps the best system is the last backed up with some hand extinguishers since it enables some investigation as to the size and nature of the problem before flooding the compartment with the extinguishing medium.

A word on installation should perhaps be directed to accessibility. Some manufacturers have done a great deal to improve the accessibility of engine-mounted ancillary components but problems may still arise on twin engine installations and thought needs to be given to elbow room for servicing and repair when planning the job. Unless the boat is beamy one engine is very likely to suffer in this respect to some extent. Forethought will save later frustration.

With diesel engines it is generally desirable to have some sound installation around the engine compartment, or even to consider a sound-containing nacelle within a larger engineroom, but in the latter case precautions must be taken to ensure that the requirements for engine environment as discussed earlier are still fully met.

An aspect of installation which is now being considered rather more than hitherto is electrolytic corrosion. If an engine is being put into either a new or an old hull it is worthwhile ensuring that the sterngear is properly bonded to a sacrificial anode of adequate size. Apart from the galvanic action due to the use of different of metals or alloys in the construction of the hull or in its underwater fittings, in a powered boat there will probably also be small differences of potential raised by rotating masses in the engine and the gearbox; there may also be stray leakages of current from electrical equipment. Without cathodic protection the overall effect can cause expensive wastage of vulnerable components – erosion of the propeller blades included – in which case there are other losses in train. A slight deterioration in blade surface finish can reduce performance by a disproportionate amount.

The best answer to all the possibilities is to make sure that all electrical equipment is properly bonded and that there are no paths via dampness or condensation for stray currents. A sacrificial anode or anodes should be fitted to the exterior hull (the makers will recommend), and this should be bonded through to the sterntube. For an installation with a rubber flexible shaft coupling the gearbox should be bonded also by wiring it to the sterntube. Thus a circuit is set up, with the current leaving the sacrificial anode (which corrodes), passing through the seawater electrolyte, and returning via the propeller and shaft, which are protected.

Appendix

SPEED COMPARISON

km/h	mph	metres/sec	knots
10	6.22	2.78	5.40
20	12.4	5.56	10.8
30	18.7	8.34	16.2
40	24.9	11.1	21.6
50	31.1	13.9	27.0
60	37.4	16.7	32.4
70	43.6	19.4	37.8
80	49.8	22.2	43.2
90	56.0	25.0	48.6
100	62.2	27.8	54.0
120	74.7	33.3	64.8
140	87.1	38.9	75.6
160	99.5	44.5	86.4
180	112	50.0	97.2
200	124	55.6	108
220	137	61.2	119
240	149	66.7	130
260	162	72.3	140
280	174	77.8	151
300	187	83.4	162

1 statute mile = 1609 m
1 nautical mile = 1852 m
1 knot = 1 nautical mile per hour

TONNAGE AND DISPLACEMENT

Ships

Deadweight tons = Cargo capacity = Max. weight of cargo on board stated in long tons (1 long ton = 1.016 metric tons).

Registered tons = (1 ton = 100 cubic feet = 2.83 cubic metres) stated in the form of both gross registered tons and net registered tons.

Gross registered tonnage = the combined volume of all spaces on board the ship.

Net registered tonnage = the cargo space available.

Displacement = the total weight of the vessel, normally used only in connection with warships.

Pleasure craft

Displacement = total weight of the boat stated in kg or metric tons of 2240.6 lbs, or short tons of 2000 lbs (USA), or long tons of 2240 lbs (Great Britain).

TM = Thames Measurement is stated in tons but is not a figure of displacement. It is merely a comparison factor between the sizes of various sailing boat types and is based on overall length and beam measurements.

$$TM = \frac{(L - B) \times B \times \frac{1}{2}B}{94}$$

Where L = length and B = beam, both in feet.

1 short ton = 2000 lbs = 0.907 metric tons
1 long ton = 2240 lbs = 1.016 metric tons
1 metric ton = 2204 lbs = 1000 kg

WEIGHTS AND MEASURES

For conversion of Imperial weights and measures to metric units multiply by the factors below.

Length

Millimeters to inches	0.03937	Inches to millimeters	25.4
Centimetres to inches	0.3937	Inches to centimetres	2.54
Metres to feet	3.281	Feet to metres	0.3048
Kilometres to miles	0.6214	Miles to kilometres	1.609

Area

| Square metres to square feet | 10.76 | Square feet to square metres | 0.0929 |
| Square kilometres to square miles | 0.3861 | Square miles to square kilometres | 2.59 |

Volume

Litres to pints (Imp)	1.76	Pints (Imp) to litres	0.568
Litres to gallons (Imp)	0.220	Gallons (Imp) to litres	4.546
Litres to pints (US)	2.12	Pints (US) to litres	0.472
Litres to gallons (US)	0.264	Gallons (US) to litres	3.785
Cubic metres to cubic feet	35.31	Cubic feet to cubic metres	0.02832

Weights

Grams to ounces	0.03527	Ounces to grams	28.35
Kilograms to pounds	2.205	Pounds to kilograms	0.4536
Kilograms to long tons	0.00084	Long tons to kilograms	1016

METRIC CONVERSION

Corresponding units

1 mile	1.609 km
1 nautical mile	1.852 km
1 cable length	0.185 km
1 fathom	1.829 m
1 yard (yd)	0.914 m
1 foot (ft)	0.305 m
1 inch (in)	25.4 mm
1 square inch (sq in)	6.452 cm^2
1 square foot (sq ft)	0.093 m^2
1 square yard (sq yd)	0.836 m^2
1 cubic inch (cu in)	16.39 cm^3
1 cubic foot (cu ft)	0.02832 m^3
1 cubic yard (cu yd)	0.765 m^3
1 Imp. gallon	4.546 litres
1 Imp. pint	0.568 litres
1 US gallon	3.785 litres
1 US pint	0.472 litres
1 ounce (oz.)	28.35 grams
1 pound (lb)	0.454 kg
1 pound-foot (lb ft)	0.138 kgm
1 mile per hour (mph)	1.609 km/hour
1 Imp. gallon/mile	282.5 litres/100 km
1 US gallon/mile	235.2 litres/100 km

Corresponding units

1 km	0.621 miles
1 nautical mile	6076 feet
1 cable length	608 feet
1 fathom	6 feet
1 m	1.094 yards
1 m	3.281 feet
1 cm	0.394 inches
1 cm^2	0.155 sq in
1 m^2	10.76 sq ft
1 m^2	1196 sq yd
1 cm^3	0.061 cu in
1 m^3	35.315 cu ft
1 m^3	1.307 cu yd
1 litre	0.219 Imp. gallon
1 litre	1.761 Imp. pints
1 litre	0.264 US gallon
1 litre	2.119 US pints
1 kg	35.27 ounces
1 kg	2.205 pounds
1 kgm	7.233 lb ft
1 km/hour	0.621 mph
10 litres/100 km	0.035 Imp. gallons/mile
10 litres/100 km	0.042 US gallons/mile

Horsepower standards

SAE = maximum output on the shaft when the engine is only fitted with the components essential for its function = gross output.
DIN = maximum output on the shaft with all standard ancillaries connected to engines as when it is installed = net output = braked output (bhp) = shaft output (shp).

Power measurement

With complete use of metric units this will be quoted in kilowatts instead of metric horsepower or the British/American brake horsepower.

1 bhp = 1.014 metric horsepower which may be given as PS (Pferdestarke), CV (Cheval Vapeur) or HK (Håstkraft).
1 metric hp = 0.735 kW
or
1 kW = 1.36 PS, CV or HK
1 PS = 0.986 bhp

Torque
For conversion of lbs ft to kgm see table.

Fuel consumption
pts/bhp hr × 1.25 = lbs/bhp hr

lbs/bhp hr × 454 = grams or millilitres/bhp hr